THE SPECTRUM OF CHILD ABUSE

Assessment, Treatment,
and Prevention

**BRUNNER/MAZEL
BASIC PRINCIPLES INTO PRACTICE SERIES
VOLUME 8**

THE SPECTRUM OF CHILD ABUSE

Assessment, Treatment, and Prevention

R. KIM OATES, M.D.

Routledge
Taylor & Francis Group
New York   London

First published by BRUNNER/ MAZEL Philadelphia and London

This edition published 2012 by Routledge

Routledge   Routledge
Taylor & Francis Group   Taylor & Francis Group
711 Third Avenue   27 Church Road
New York, NY 10017   Hove, East Sussex BN3 2FA

Library of Congress Cataloging-in-Publication Data

Oates, Kim.
    The spectrum of child abuse: assessment, treatment, and prevention
/ R. Kim Oates.
        p. cm. — (Brunner/Mazel basic principles into practice series; v.8)
    Includes bibliographical references and index.
    ISBN 0-87630-807-8 (paper)   ISBN 978-0-87630-807-3
    1. Child abuse. 2. Abused children. I. Title. II. Series.
HV6626.5.037   1996
362.7'6—dc20   96-17678
                                                         CIP

CONTENTS

FOREWORD

Why should any of us want to learn about the spectrum of child abuse? Why should we be concerned about its prevention, identification, and treatment?

Every year, throughout every country in the world, children, many, many children—in the millions—are physically, sexually, and emotionally abused and neglected by their own parents or guardians. Literally thousands of these children die as a result; most of those who die never reach their first birthday. And for those who survive the abuses, both the immediate and long-term scars of the abuse are significant and severe. Some of the scars are physical, some developmental, and some psychological. Yet, all can interfere with a child's ability to grow into a healthy and productive adult.

Child abuse is often described as the linchpin or source of so many other social problems—dropping out of school, juvenile delinquency, substance abuse, violent behavior directed either at oneself or at others, and even subsequent difficulties with parenting. The institutional costs of child abuse are enormous as society responds with medical, legal, social, and educational interventions. So, too, are the social and emotional costs. To save lives, to avoid physical and emotional suffering, and even to save resources—these are the reasons why we all must be concerned about child abuse and why we must learn what we can about how to identify, treat, and prevent it.

The search for answers to all that is included in the spectrum of child abuse is not an easy endeavor, and those who seek simple explanations and easy answers will be sorely disappointed. As this book makes clear, we are talking about a very complex set of problems, with myriad explanations, requiring a variety of coordinated and multidisciplinary responses. And often the explanations we seek will not yet have been determined, at least scientifically. So what can this book offer?

Throughout the chapters of this book, the reader will find solid information about the different types of child abuse, the underlying causes, as well as the sequelae and methods of detection, prevention, and treatment. The chapters together form an important and full compilation of what we are comfortable saying "is known" about child abuse; as such, the chapters form a basic textbook on one of society's most cruel and complex problems. Guided by the information contained here, the concerned professional will have a good road map to understanding much of the "what" and the "why" of child abuse. It will be in the application of that new found knowledge in real world situations with real families in real communities that the professional will confront the limitations of this road map.

Let the reader not be deceived, however, by the knowledge presented in this book. Although we do know a tremendous amount about the disturbing issue of child abuse, we must still recognize that it is also a very complex issue. So the reader hoping to digest this text in order to be armed with black-and-white answers will find, with the first and subsequent cases of suspected child abuse, that answers come in gray, rather than black and white.

We also need to acknowledge that a lot remains to be learned about this issue. Even as this book, which compiles the latest research findings on the topic, goes to press, dozens and dozens of our colleagues around the world are engaged in new studies that will result in an expanded knowledge base. The reader hoping to use this book as *the* definitive text on the issue of child abuse will soon realize the need to continually supplement the material presented here with new information that can be gleaned only by dedicated scouring of the now many professional journals on this topic.

In all likelihood, if child abuse were not such a complex problem, we would have long since reduced its incidence, and perhaps we would even be setting target dates—as one might with other public health diseases—for its eradication. Nevertheless, if child abuse were not such a complex problem, you would probably not have been drawn to this book and would not be keen to learn more about it.

As you embark upon an exploration of childhood's most heinous side, and as you seek to apply what you learn in these pages, do know that it will not be easy. But do know that the effort is well worth it. Armed with the information here and that which you will seek elsewhere, you will have the very real opportunity to help ensure that it shouldn't hurt to be a child.

Anne Cohn Donnelly, D.P.H.
Executive Director
National Committee to Prevent Child Abuse

PREFACE

When I was asked to write a book on child abuse for the Basic Principles Into Practice series, my initial reaction was, "Not another book on child abuse." There has been a plethora of books on various aspects of child abuse—and as the person responsible for organizing book reviews for the journal *Child Abuse and Neglect,* I have seen most of them. Among them were some very good books indeed and it appeared that the area already was pretty well covered.

On further reflection, however, I realized that many of these books had been written for a particular professional group and that the majority covered only one aspect of abuse, such as sexual abuse or physical abuse. This is not surprising. So much knowledge is available about the various aspects of child abuse that therapists often specialize in, and write about, just one area of abuse. Very few books offer an overview of the entire spectrum of child abuse so that I concluded, there likely is room for "yet another book on child abuse."

In this book I have attempted to present an overview of physical abuse, sexual abuse, emotional abuse, and neglect, looking at the historical awareness of these problems, their incidence and epidemiology, contributing factors, assessment, treatment, and prevention. To do this within the confines of one book means that the topics are not covered in depth, but rather are given enough attention to provide what I hope is a balanced perspective on them, supported by research findings from around the world.

The book is not aimed at any one professional group, but should be a useful introduction for all those wanting to learn about child abuse, including the motivated lay person. It should also be of use to professionals already working in this area who need an overview of the subject of child abuse.

The abuse of children is one of the most important problems that confronts society, not only because of the harm it does to children, but also because of the long-term effect it has on those children in their adult relationships. Sometimes, the problem seems so great that professionals become disenchanted when they see how much there is to do. When this happens, it is helpful to look back at how much progress has been made. Abused children are now identified because we have learned how to recognize them. There are many good treatment programs. Prevention is being emphasized. Many children are now being helped whereas in the past their problem would not even have been recognized. There is certainly much more to do, but glancing back occasionally can give encouragement to press on.

I am grateful to my friends and colleagues from around the world, many of whom have worked with me in the International Society for the Prevention of Child Abuse and Neglect and many more who have encouraged me and supported me professionally. Particular thanks go to my wife, Robyn, and my children, Matthew, Peter, and Sarah, who always manage to help me keep my feet on the ground when my head starts to get into the clouds.

THE SPECTRUM OF CHILD ABUSE

Assessment, Treatment,
and Prevention

1

THE DEFINITION OF CHILD ABUSE AND NEGLECT

Almost daily, we are confronted by newspaper reports, magazine articles or television programs describing child abuse. What is child abuse and why is there so much media attention? Is child abuse increasing? Are reports exaggerated? Can we believe what children say? What do we know about the perpetrators of abuse? What happens to abused children—will some become abusers when they grow up? How can abused children be treated? How can scarce resources be best used? How can we reduce the incidence of child abuse? These are typical of the questions that the public, as well as professionals, often ask. Unfortunately, there are no simple answers. Child abuse is a complex problem and complex problems rarely have a simple solution.

This book is an introduction to the problem of child abuse. While it may not be possible to answer all of the above questions fully, much has been learned about the subject. The aim of this book is to provide an understanding of the problem based on current knowledge, as well as to provide references for those who wish to pursue the topic further.

THE SPECTRUM OF CHILD ABUSE

Child abuse can be divided into four broad areas:

- Physical abuse
- Sexual abuse
- Neglect and nonorganic failure to thrive
- Emotional abuse

These are not clear-cut categories. Although in many cases a child will suffer from only one of these types of abuse, for others, the abuse may include two or more of these varieties. And for some, what started as neglect in the first year of life may manifest as another form of abuse, such as physical abuse, in the toddler period. It is common for children to be subjected to more than one type of abuse, particularly when emotional abuse is included, with possibly less than 5% of cases involving only one type (Ney, Fung, & Wickett, 1994). However, for ease of discussion, the four areas of abuse will be considered separately.

PHYSICAL ABUSE

Definition

A simple, early definition of a physically abused child provided by Kempe and Helfer (1972) is still useful:

> Any child who receives nonaccidental physical injury as a result of acts, or omissions on the part of his parents or guardians. (p. xi)

This definition has the advantage of recognizing the vulnerability of the child and of placing responsibility on the child's caretaker. It also points out that most physical abuse is caused by people who have responsibility for the care of the child. However, there is no universally accepted definition, which complicates the task of understanding the epidemiology of child abuse in all of its forms. Definitions vary considerably. For example, Swedish law bans all forms of physical punishment and other injurious or humiliating treatment of children. On the other hand, Straus's survey of child abuse in the United States (1980a) used a definition that excluded the "normal" violence of family life, such as pushing, slapping, and throwing objects, but included acts that put the child at risk of serious injury, such as kicking, biting, punching, hitting with an object, or using a knife or gun.

Problems with definitions occur because children's rights evolve over time. What is acceptable in one society may not be acceptable in another and what was regarded as normal in previous generations may be considered unacceptable now. Also, if one simply looks at the physical injuries, the problem in the family may be missed altogether. Physical injuries often depend on the circumstances surrounding the violent act.

A child may be pushed roughly to the floor by his father. He first lands against a soft armchair and then falls to the carpeted floor. No injuries are sustained.

On another occasion, exactly the same amount of force and aggression is used by the same father. This time the child hits his head on a protruding cupboard, sustains a fracture, and then falls to a concrete floor, receiving further head injuries.

In the second incident, the child will present for medical care and is likely to be diagnosed as abused. In the first episode, the boy would not present for medical attention at all. These two scenarios involving the same amount of force and aggression emphasize that the *act* of violence on the part of the parent is more important than the visible injury.

The physical injury is best thought of as a physical sign of an underlying problem. To use a medical analogy, when a child comes to a physician with a skin rash, the rash presents the physician with a physical sign that there may be an underlying problem. It is the physician's job to consider all the possible causes and to do a thorough assessment. In some cases, the rash may simply be a sign of a mild viral infection. In other cases, it may signify a life-threatening disease. Similarly, in child abuse, the physical injury is the outward sign of an underlying problem and calls for a thorough assessment of the child's family and environment. It is the result of this assessment that will show how the problem can best be managed and the child protected.

Historical Background

Society sometimes pays only lip service to the concept that children are our most precious resource and that they need to be loved, nurtured, and protected. In historical terms, this is a relatively new concept for society as a whole, in contrast to individual families. The psychohistorian Lloyd De Mause (1974) starts his book on the history of childhood with these sentences:

> The history of childhood is a nightmare from which we have only recently begun to awaken. The further back in history one goes, the lower the level of child care and the more likely children are to be killed, abandoned, beaten, terrorized and abused. (p. 1).

It is not surprising then that child abuse has been an integral part of children's fairy tales, such as *Hansel and Gretel,* and of nursery rhymes, such as this well-known example:

> There was an old women who lived in a shoe. She had so many children she did not know what to do. She

gave them some broth without any bread, and whipped them all soundly and put them to bed.

Even the much-loved puppet show *Punch and Judy* tells how Judy gives Mr. Punch her baby to mind. At first Mr. Punch rocks the baby on his knee. The baby begins to cry. Mr. Punch responds by rocking the baby harder and, eventually, violently. The crying persists. Mr. Punch then loses control, hits the baby, and throws it out of the window to its death.

Various forms of child abuse have been documented and sometimes condoned in the past. Many cultures used infanticide as an acceptable method of family planning and to dispose of weak, premature, or deformed infants (Bakan, 1971). Sometimes, children were killed for superstitious reasons as it was believed that slain infants would benefit the sterile woman, kill disease, and confer health, vigor, and youthfulness. To ensure durability of important buildings, children were sometimes buried under the foundations (Radbill, 1974). In England, during the industrial revolution in the mideighteenth century, children from poor families provided industry with a cheap work force. Children as young as 5 years of age worked in factories for up to 14 hours each day and often suffered additional cruel treatment during this time. A movement for child labor reform, by Robert Owen and Sir Robert Peel, led to passing the Factory Act by the English Parliament in 1802. However, this Act protected only poor children who had been separated from their parents from being forced to work in appalling conditions in the factories, and did not apply to children still living with their parents. These parents were still legally entitled to send their children to work in factories and to collect their children's wages.

Infanticide was common in England as late as the nineteenth century. In London, 80 percent of illegitimate children who were sent out to wet nurses died, often because they would be killed by the wet nurses, who would continue to collect the nursing fees (Fraser, 1976). Newborn children could be insured for about one English pound under a "burial club" insurance policy. If the child died, the parents could claim between three and five pounds in insurance, which meant that some parents killed their infants or had someone else kill them in order to claim the insurance (Fraser, 1976).

It was not until the late nineteenth century that moves to protect children from abuse began to have some influence. The story of 10-year-old Mary Ellen Wilson in 1874 was a landmark case. Mary Ellen, who had been abandoned by her mother, was beaten and mistreated by her foster parents. Mrs. Wheeler, a church caseworker in the neighborhood, became aware of Mary Ellen's plight. However, the efforts to try to protect Mary Ellen were fruitless. Although there were laws to protect children, there apparently were no means of legal intervention for children living at home. In desperation, Mrs. Wheeler appealed to Henry Bergh, the founder of the American Society for the Prevention of Cruelty to Animals, who was famous for his dramatic rescue of mistreated horses in the streets of New York. Mrs. Wheeler approached Bergh with the contention that Mary Ellen was a member of the animal kingdom. Bergh took the case, which was heard in the New York Supreme Court and resulted in Mary Ellen being removed from her foster parents. She eventually lived with Mrs. Wheeler's family, seemed to recover from her traumatic childhood, was successful as a mother, and lived for 92 years.

As a result of the Mary Ellen case, Henry Bergh, along with Elbridge Gerry, the lawyer in the case, founded the New York Society for the Prevention of Cruelty to Children, the first organization of its kind in the United States (Stevens & Eide, 1990; Lazoritz, 1990). In 1881, an English banker, T. F. Agnew, visited the New York society and was so impressed that, on his return to Liverpool, he established England's first Society for the Prevention of Cruelty to Children in 1883 (Allen & Morton, 1961).

A French physician was the first to describe the medical features of child abuse. Ambrose Tardieu's study of 32 children who had died as a result of abuse (Tardieu, 1860) clearly described not only the medical findings, but also the demographic, social, and psychiatric features of this condition. However, most members of the medical profession had little awareness of the size of the problem.

For example, the American radiologist John Caffey (1946), reported what appeared to be a new syndrome in 1946. He described six children with subdural hematomas who also had multiple long-bone fractures. Some of these children had other injuries, as well, such as bruising and retinal hemorrhages. Some were reported as being undernourished and developmentally delayed. Caffey could not find any evidence of underlying skeletal disease and concluded that the fractures were most likely of traumatic origin. Although he was unable to obtain a history of trauma from the parents, he pointed out that negligence may have been a factor.

The features of child abuse were also slow to be recognized on the other side of the Atlantic. An English orthopedic surgeon (Astley, 1953) described six children with normal bone structure who had metaphyseal fractures. Some of these children were also noted to have bruising, retinal detachment, and bilateral black eyes. The parents were described as normal, sensible individuals who gave no history of trauma. Despite the associated soft tissue injuries, Astley did not appear to consider trauma as a cause but labeled the findings as a new condition, "metaphyseal fragility of bones."

Radiologist F. N. Silverman (1953) provided a more perceptive answer. He described three children with unusual fractures involving the metaphyseal region and wrote that an adequate history of trauma for fractures of this nature could be obtained by careful questioning of the parents. An important contribution to understanding the cause of these injuries was made by Woolley and Evans in 1955. They reviewed earlier radiological studies and emphasized the traumatic nature of these findings, pointing out that the environments of these incidents were often hazardous and undesirable. However, even as late as 1955, society was not yet ready to accept that parents could intentionally injure their children. Woolley and Evans had to use a euphemism, stating that they believed the children had been subjected to "undesirable vectors of force" (Woolley & Evans, 1955).

Widespread recognition came in the 1960s, but not without difficulty. In 1960, Henry Kempe, professor of pediatrics at the University of Colorado, submitted a paper on child abuse to the American Academy of Pediatrics Scientific Meeting, only to have it rejected. The next year, Kempe was elected chairman of the program committee for the Academy and organized a seminar on child abuse at the Academy meeting (Steele, 1993). The following year, Kempe and colleagues (1962) published some of the data presented at this seminar in the landmark paper, "The Battered Child." The authors concluded that physical abuse was a significant cause of death and injury among children and suggested that psychiatric factors were likely to be of importance in understanding the disorder. The intense interest in child abuse at a political and media level can be dated from the appearance of this paper. Within 10 years, every state in the United States had enacted laws about child abuse notification.

Child physical abuse is now accepted as one of the more serious problems of childhood, although the denial of its extent and existence, which resulted in its being so slow to be recognized, still exists. Denial can be a problem for some members of the medical profession, ranging from a disbelief that parents actually can injure their children to not wanting to become involved because recognition may mean reporting and reporting may mean going to court. Some may be reluctant to do more than treat the injury because they erroneously believe that doctor–patient confidentiality may be compromised. At times, there is a tendency to identify with the parents, particularly when the abuser is of a similar professional standing and ethnic background or may not fit the professional stereotype of what a "child abuser" is like. The fact is that child physical abuse is common and should be considered when unexplained or unlikely injuries occur.

Incidence

Although we do not know the incidence of physical abuse, we do know that most abuse occurs within the privacy of the child's home and that as most abusers give a false explanation of injuries that come to medical attention, the reported incidence of physical abuse is underestimated. We also know that not all reports of abuse are genuine. Some may be malicious, while others may be reports of actual abuse that cannot to be substantiated. Thus, there is the situation of simultaneous underreporting of real cases and some degree of overreporting. The reported incidence for all forms of child abuse in the United States was 2,989,000 cases in 1993, of which 1,016,000 cases were substantiated, giving a rate of 15 cases of substantiated abuse per 1000 children. Physical abuse accounted for 25% of these cases, a rate of just under four cases of substantiated physical abuse per 1000 children (Daro & McCurdy, 1993).

The most recent figures from Australia, with a total population of 17 million, show that 49,721 cases were reported over 12 months with 20,868 (42%) of these reports being substantiated, a rate of 4.2 substantiated reports per 1000 children. Twenty-six percent of these cases were physical abuse (Angus & Wilkinson, 1993).

Although the various incidence studies have problems in sampling and in reporter bias, the important message is that physical abuse is much more common than other serious disorders of childhood, for example, cystic fibrosis (1 in 2500 births), acute childhood leukemia (annual incidence of 1 in 30,000), and juvenile diabetes (1 in every 1000 school-aged children).

SEXUAL ABUSE

Definition

A widely used definition of child sexual abuse is:

> The involvement of dependent, developmentally im-
> mature children and adolescents in sexual activities
> which they do not fully comprehend, are unable to
> give informed consent to, and that violate social taboos
> of family roles. (Schechter & Roberge, 1976, p. 129)

An important point in this definition is that the child's
consent is not informed. Children may consent to sexual
relations with adults, often just because of fear and threats.
This consent is not freely given and certainly is not informed, as the children are unaware of the significance of
their actions.

Sgroi's definition (1982) emphasizes the power relationship between the perpetrator and the victim, pointing out
that the child has no choice:

> Child sexual abuse is a sexual act imposed on a child
> who lacks emotional, maturational and cognitive de-
> velopment. The ability to lure a child into a sexual
> relationship is based upon the all-powerful and domi-
> nant position of the adult or older adolescent perpe-
> trator, which is in sharp contrast to the child's age
> dependency and subordinate position. Authority and
> power enable the perpetrator, implicitly or directly, to
> coerce the child into sexual compliance (p. 9)

Differences in definition create difficulties when one is
comparing different incidence studies, particularly when
some definitions have different upper age levels for the
child (e.g., 12 or 16 years) and some are restricted to sexual
abuse by family members. Most investigators exclude
sexual play between children of similar ages and include a

requirement for there to be an age difference of 5 years or more between the two individuals. Probably, the simpler the definition, the better (Fraser, 1981):

Sexual abuse is the exploitation of a child for the sexual gratification of an adult. (p. 58)

Historical Background

Sexual exploitation of children by adults is not new. What is new is the professional and public awareness of a problem that has been present for many centuries. In the Roman empire, boy-brothels were popular in many cities. Anal intercourse with young boys, preferably castrated, was common, and this act was depicted on erotic vases. Boys were sometimes castrated for the express purpose of their being used in a brothel. Castration was not only performed for sexual reasons, but also as treatment for a variety of childhood illnesses or so that the testicles could be used for magical purposes (De Mause, 1974).

Sexual abuse was also common in the Greek empire. Athens had a rent-a-boy service. The sexual abuse of pupils by their private tutors was so prevalent that Athens had laws to prevent teachers from being alone or in the dark with their boy pupils. Sexual abuse of girls was also common historically. In some cultures, daughters were lent to guests as an act of hospitality, and children as young as 11 years old served in houses of prostitution, according to the records of the London Society for the Protection of Young Females (Radbill, 1980).

By the time the New World had been settled, sexual prohibitions were becoming stricter. In Connecticut in 1672, the penalty set by the court for incest in one case was for the daughter to be whipped and the father to be executed (Illick, 1974). This was a clear instance of blaming the victim, an attitude still occasionally encountered today. Even in Victorian England, with its outwardly strict morality, child prostitution was rife, particularly because of the widespread belief that intercourse with a child would cure venereal disease. Female child prostitutes frequented the streets of London, often in the guise of flower sellers. Child sexual abuse was documented in France by Tardieu, who reported 60 cases of sexual offenses against young girls (Radbill, 1980). In 1839, a police commissary in Paris devoted one chapter of his annual report to the sexual abuse of children (Beraud, 1839).

In his early work, Freud was aware of the importance of sexual abuse, writing in 1896 in the *Etiology of Hysteria*:

> I therefore put forward the thesis that at the bottom of every case of hysteria, there are one or more occurrences of premature sexual experiences, occurrences which belong to the earliest years of childhood. (p. 203)

This view was not well received by his peers (Masson, 1984), and 10 years later, Freud revised his theory to be more acceptable to his colleagues and to the culture of his time.

There was little further discussion of sexual abuse in the scientific literature. When it was mentioned, it was explained away. Kinsey's (1953) study of sexual behavior in females showed that 9% of the sample recalled sexual contact with an adult before their 14th birthday. Although Kinsey's work was given considerable publicity, this aspect of it received little attention—perhaps because of the public's denial of the taboo of child sexual abuse or because Kinsey and coworkers played down the significance of this finding (Russell, 1984).

Child sexual abuse was not widely discussed until the late 1970s. It is logical that this recognition could only follow the recognition of physical abuse. Once the public and professionals began to realize that parents could seriously injure their own children physically, it became possible to recognize the even greater taboo of child sexual abuse with the realization that much of this occurs within the child's own family (Kempe, 1978).

It is worth asking why recognition of this problem took so long. For a long period, families and professionals had protected themselves and their feelings by pretending that sexual abuse was rare and something that only involved "other people." When sexual abuse of children was referred to, it was usually in the media and involved lurid, often violent episodes of stranger assault. The regular and persistent abuse of children in their own homes, by people on whom they were dependent and whom they should have been able to trust, was not mentioned, mainly because discussion of sexual abuse within a family can be a threat to the very structure of that family. As inadequate as some family relationships may be, they are often all the family has. In the past, when a child did tell someone of the abuse, the child was often not believed or was even punished for making such an outrageous suggestion. For those parents who listened to their children and became concerned enough to take the child to the doctor, the claim was often dismissed by the professional as the result of a vivid juvenile imagination. Professionals complied in the denial of this problem because they had no experience or training in the area and because it was often too uncomfortable for them.

Persistence by a relatively small number of professionals and by sections of the feminist movement, along with increased media awareness, has brought child sexual abuse more into the open, although the level of denial still remains high for some. Many are reluctant to believe that anyone, especially someone who appears to be normal, could abuse a child sexually. This reluctance leads to taking refuge in questioning the child's credibility, reliability, and motives, even shifting blame to the child and thus reinforcing the stereotype that a real child molester is someone who is a sinister stranger—not at all like our friends or family (Summitt, 1990).

Incidence and Epidemiology

One hears so many reports in the media, as well as in the scientific literature, about the large number of sexual abuse cases that some definitions of the terms used are needed to help interpret this information.

The *incidence* of sexual abuse in children is the number of new cases that occur each year divided by the total population of children. We do not know the true incidence because many cases go unreported. We can obtain information about the *reported incidence* from reporting agencies, although these figures are hard to compare with each other as different agencies may use different definitions of sexual abuse or different upper age limits, both factors that would strongly influence the reported incidence.

The *prevalence* of child sexual abuse is the number of people in the population who have been sexually abused as children. Prevalence studies in which populations of adults are asked about sexual abuse in their childhood have given figures ranging widely from 6% to 62% (Peters, Wyatt, & Finkelhor, 1986). These differences reflect some of the problems in prevalence studies, such as the source of the sample (in terms of education, socioeconomic status, and ethnicity); the broadness or the narrowness of the definition used in the survey; the upper age used for defining the person as a child (some investigators have used 18 years, others have used 14 years); the method of the questioning about the abuse (by mail, by face-to-face interview, by telephone, or as part of a larger survey); the sampling technique (random sample, college students, community sample, sex of respondents); the response rate; and the accuracy of the respondent's memory.

The high figures from these prevalence studies are in contrast to studies of reported incidence, which tend to give much lower figures. For example, the reported incidence of sexual abuse in the United States in 1993 was 5 cases per 1000 children, with the incidence of substantiated cases being just over 2 cases per 1000 children (Daro

& McCurdy, 1993). In Australia, the reported incidence of child sexual abuse is 2.5 cases per 1000 children, with substantiated reports of 1 case per 1000 children (Angus & Wilkinson, 1993). Whatever flaws there may be in the methodology of prevalence studies or in the analysis of notification figures, the vast difference between reported incidence and prevalence confirms the view that most child sexual abuse goes unreported.

NEGLECT AND NONORGANIC FAILURE TO THRIVE

Two aspects of child abuse, neglect and nonorganic failure to thrive, have been somewhat ignored by professionals and the media (Wolock & Horowitz, 1984). Physical abuse and sexual abuse are active events that often have obvious consequences. These forms of abuse suggest an urgency to treat, protect, and prevent. Neglect is more insidious. It is not well defined, does not need sophisticated high technology to make the diagnosis, and rarely produces the outrage that may accompany reports of physical or sexual abuse. Nevertheless, it is an important part of the spectrum of child abuse and often has serious long-term consequences, not only for the child but also for that child's parenting skills as an adult.

Neglect

Definition and Incidence

Children have a number of basic needs. These include the needs for love and security, opportunities, new experiences, praise, recognition, and responsibility, as well as for adequate food, housing, clothing, medical care, and education. Neglect is usually regarded as the failure of parents to provide these things, particularly the material items. Because neglect is so difficult to define and because definitions vary, it is difficult to be sure of its incidence. In the United States, the incidence of reported child neglect in 1993 was 15 cases per 1000 children with seven cases per 1000 children being substantiated (Daro & McCurdy, 1993). The reported incidence of substantiated cases in Australia was one confirmed case per 1000 children (Angus & Wilkinson, 1993), the large difference in numbers between these countries most likely due being in part to differences in definition.

Neglect can take various forms. Schmitt (1981) defines five types of neglect: medical neglect, safety neglect, educational neglect, physical neglect, and emotional deprivation. These will be discussed in more detail in Chapter 5.

Nonorganic Failure to Thrive

Definition

Some infants whose needs for adequate nutrition and emotional stimulation are neglected develop nonorganic failure to thrive. Although commonly used, the term is an unsatisfactory one, since it is a description, not a diagnosis. It is rather like saying that the child's diagnosis is "a cough," without giving the underlying reason why the child has a cough. Also, there is no widely accepted definition of failure to thrive. A review of 22 current reference texts and 13 recent journal articles on failure to thrive shows that they lack consensus in their criteria for this condition (Wilcox, et al., 1989).

Despite the lack of a clear definition, the term "failure to thrive" is used to describe an infant who shows a decline from a previously established growth pattern. It is sometimes reserved for infants whose failure to gain weight places them below the third percentile for their age. Linear growth may also be affected, although usually to a lesser extent. There may be evidence of delay in psychomotor development. When the history is suggestive of emotional or nutritional deprivation or both, the condition is often termed nonorganic failure to thrive. The implication is that the child's social, emotional, or nutritional environment is disturbed to the point where it interferes with normal growth and development.

Growth failure cannot be strictly defined as organic or nonorganic, as in the nonorganic variety there may sometimes be a contributing organic factor. A reasonable definition of growth failure, where the problem is primarily one of parenting ("nonorganic failure to thrive"), is:

> Failure to maintain a previously established growth pattern which responds to a combination of providing for the infant's nutritional and emotional needs (Oates, 1984, p. 95)

Historical Background

Growth failure was first noted to be associated with emotional deprivation in children living in institutions where death rates were high. The severity of this problem was brought to attention in 1915 by Henry Chapin, who reported on 11 "infant asylums" (the term used for institutions that cared for infants) in different parts of the United States. For children under two years of age living in these institutions, the death rate was 42% (Chapin, 1915a). Chapin called the problem "the cachexia of hospitalization." He suggested that it resulted from a combination of a poor physical environment and a lack of individual care and nurturing in the institution (Chapin, 1915b). Chapin contrasted the mortality in institutions with the results of the Speedwell Society, an organization that took infants from institutions and fostered them with carefully selected private families where the foster mother could be instructed in feeding and caring for the baby. The mortality rate among these infants was much lower than for those kept in institutions. Probably, Chapin's most important observation was that in some cases the condition of these infants was due to a problem in parenting, noting that fathers played an important role.

This concern for infants in institutions did not attract much attention until 1945 with the observations of Spitz, who reported anaclitic depression, malnutrition, and growth failure in infants under one year of age kept in foundling homes (Spitz, 1945). Spitz suggested that lack of emotional stimulation, rather than nutritional deprivation, was the main reason for the depression and growth failure.

It was not only in foundling homes where infants became withdrawn and had poor growth. In the days when children were kept in the hospital for long periods, sometimes with active discouragement of parental visiting, the same features could be seen. Bakwin (1949) described the characteristic features of these children:

> The hospitalized infant is thin and pale....The facial expression is unhappy and gives an impression of misery. Muscle tone is poor and it is possible to extend the legs fully at the knees, contrasting in this way with normal young infants. There is no alteration in deep reflexes. The infant shows no interest in his environment, lying quietly in bed, rarely crying and moving very little. Such movements as he makes are slow and deliberate, unlike the quick movements one expects at this age (p. 512).

Bakwin recommended that the mother should stay with the baby as much as possible whenever the baby was hospitalized for a prolonged period. This view, while obvious today, was a revolutionary one at the time.

Following the recognition of the dangers of emotional deprivation leading to failure to thrive in institutions and hospitals, it was realized that the clinical syndrome of growth failure secondary to emotional deprivation could also occur in children living in their own homes (Coleman & Provence, 1957).

Nonorganic failure to thrive or growth failure where the problem is primarily one of caretaking is now recognized to be a complex problem in which a variety of factors can play a part to different degrees. These include environmental stresses on the family, minor medical problems in the infant that make feeding stressful or ineffective, problems of attachment, and difficulties in parenting capabilities.

Incidence

The lack of consensus in definition makes it difficult to determine the incidence of nonorganic failure to thrive, with most reporting agencies including it under the broad heading of neglect. Estimates of children admitted to hospitals with "failure to thrive" have ranged from 0.9% (English, 1978) to 5% (Shaheen et al., 1968), with 15% to 58% of these infants showing no organic cause for their growth failure (Oates & Kempe, 1996).

EMOTIONAL ABUSE

Emotional abuse tends to be the hidden form of child abuse. Yet it is at the very heart of child abuse. It has been argued that, rather than emotional abuse being the part of the spectrum of child abuse and neglect, it is the factor that underlies all other forms of abuse because of the psychological message of worthlessness and debasement that is received by children who are physically and sexually abused (Garbarino, 1989).

Definition

Emotional abuse is different from emotional neglect. Emotional *neglect* can be defined as:

A result of subtle or blatant acts of omission or commission experienced by the child, which cause handicapping stress on the child and which is manifested in patterns of inappropriate behavior (Whiting, 1976, p. 2).

This definition emphasizes the stress caused to the child, sometimes by acts of omission that are great enough to interfere with the child's normal functioning and that may result in behavior disturbances. In contrast, emotional *abuse* is an active, constant behavior toward the child, usually by a parent, where self-esteem is pulled down rather than built up. Emotional abuse is:

> The habitual, verbal harassment of a child by disparagement, criticism, threat, ridicule and the inversion of love; by verbal and nonverbal means rejection and withdrawal are substituted (Skuse, 1989, p. 692).

It is not only parents who can emotionally abuse children. Emotional abuse can be caused by relatives (especially if they are living in the family home); by neighbors; by those caring for children in institutions, detention homes, centers for the intellectually disabled, child care, and hospitals; and by schoolteachers. Emotional abuse can be caused by an adult who is in a position of power in relation to the child and who should have some responsibility for the child's welfare.

Emotional abuse by the child's own parents is likely to be more serious, although if the child has no parents or is in substitute care, emotional abuse in these circumstances can be equally serious. Emotional abuse of children is always totally unacceptable, but cultural norms have to be remembered. Behaviors that may seem abusive in some cultures could be acceptable in others and may not be harmful if they do not involve the replacement of love with rejection and withdrawal. However, when the behavior toward the child conveys a culture-specific message of rejection or when it impairs the development of a socially relevant psychological process, such as the development of self-esteem, then it is emotional abuse, whatever the family's cultural norms (Garbarino, Guttman, & Seeley, 1986).

Incidence

Because emotional abuse does not leave any physical injuries, it does not come to the attention of medical, law enforcement, or welfare authorities as frequently as the more dramatic forms of abuse. Its ongoing nature means that there is usually no crisis, such as the discovery of sexual abuse or the injuries from physical abuse, to precipitate a consultation with a person involved in child health or welfare.

The most recent figures from the United States (Daro & McCurdy, 1993) show that of the reported cases of child abuse that were substantiated, 4% were reports of emotional abuse, an incidence of 0.6 case per 1000 children. This differs from an earlier National Incidence Study (Burgdorff, 1980) which found 3.2 per 1000 children in the United States to be victims of emotional abuse and neglect. Presumably, differences in definitions account for these differing figures. Australian figures for child abuse and neglect show that 25% of reported cases are for emotional abuse, the same incidence as for sexual abuse, giving a rate of one case of substantiated emotional abuse per 1000 children. What we can be sure of from these studies is that the true incidence is considerably higher, since emotional abuse is likely to be the least recognized aspect of child abuse.

2

WHY DOES
CHILD ABUSE OCCUR?

In this chapter, some of the theories of the causation of physical and sexual abuse will be reviewed, but those hoping to find a simple explanation for the problem of abuse will be disappointed. Child abuse is a very complex problem, and complex problems rarely have simple answers. The aim of this chapter is to present some of the reasons why abuse occurs and to review some of the factors that increase the risk of abuse.

PHYSICAL ABUSE

We all know that violence in society is common. Yet, what not everyone realizes is that violence in families is also common. In many instances, it is safer to be on the streets after dark with a stranger than to be at home in the bosom of one's family, for it is in the family that many accidents, acts of violence, and murders occur. Straus (1980b) believes that humans have an inherent capacity for violence that is exacerbated by stress. This link between violence and stress was shown in a national sample of adults in the United States where stressful life experiences were shown to be associated with assaults between husband and wife, with the number of violent incidents increasing as the amount of stress increased (Straus, 1980a).

It has even been proposed that violence in the family is more common than love (Straus, Gelles, & Steinmetz, 1980). A survey of parents by Gelles (1978) in the United States found 4% of children were bitten, kicked, or punched by their parents. A gun or knife was used by 0.2% of parents. Many of the parents in this survey felt that these behaviors were acceptable methods of rearing children. The problem of violence in families is not confined to the United States and has been documented in most Western countries (Gelles & Cornell, 1990).

Although not often acknowledged, parents' feelings of intense anger toward their children are not rare. A survey of mothers interviewed one month after birth found that 61% of them admitted that there had been times when they felt angry with their babies (Graham, 1980). When mothers in Wales were asked about punishment of their children ages 1 to 4 years, 57% said that on at least one occasion they had lost their tempers completely and hit their children really hard, while 40% had entertained the fear that they might lose their temper and severely damage their children (Frude & Goss, 1980).

Many families who use corporal punishment (physical punishment inflicted on a child by an adult) would not regard this as violent behavior. Corporal punishment has been regarded as a method of discipline throughout history and is still widely used today. It is estimated that over 90% of American children ages 2 to 6 receive physical punishment as a method of discipline (Straus, 1991). Some use it because that is what their parents used on them when they were children. Others hit their children out of frustration and loss of control. Still others use it because they believe it works. It is often true that hitting a child will temporarily stop an undesirable behavior. However, it does not teach the child the expected behavior. Parents who rely on physical punishment as their only means of discipline reach a point, as their child grows older and larger, where physical punishment no longer can be used. If this is their only form of discipline (in contrast to such techniques as teaching, encouraging, rewarding and showing by example), then the parent will have little chance of influencing the child beyond a certain age.

The experience of the Scandinavian countries and Austria, where parents by law are not allowed to hit their children, suggests that societies do not break down when parents stop hitting their children. However, it must be realized that the intention of the Scandinavian legislation was education rather than punishment. Along with the legislation, there was an education campaign, helping parents to learn more acceptable methods of discipline. The legislation was not meant to punish parents, but to aim for a generation of children to grow up without the experience of being hit, so that they may in turn be less aggressive and violent in their dealings with other adults and with their own children.

Before deciding what we consider to be violent or abusive behavior, we also have to look at what other cultures regard as normal and as abusive. The Western concept of child rearing is based on a narrow slice of humanity, which can hamper our understanding of child rearing in other cultures (Korbin, 1980). Consider the following illustration:

> In London in 1974, an East African woman cut the faces of her two young sons with a razor blade and rubbed charcoal into the wounds. The woman was arrested and charged with child abuse. During the proceedings, it was learned that she was a member of a racial group that traditionally practices facial scarification. Her action had been an attempt to assert the cultural identity of her children. She knew that without these markings her boys would be unable to participate as adults when they returned to their own culture. From her point of view, failure to scarify the children would have been neglectful or abusive within the cultural context of her racial group.

This type of incident demonstrates the difficulty of comparing practices taken out of their cultural context (Korbin, 1977). As difficult as the concept of facial scarification is for Westerners to understand, this woman's community may have had similar difficulty in understanding the prolonged and often painful orthodontic work on children that our society believes is not only acceptable, but is also desirable.

Even practices regarded as normal can differ markedly among cultures. Middle-class Americans, English, and Australian families like a child to have his or her own bed, if not a separate room. This is in contrast to Hawaiian-American women who have difficulty accepting that middle-class Americans could put an infant into another bed or even a separate room. Their cultural belief suggests that this sort of practice is detrimental to child development and can be potentially dangerous. Korbin (1980) relates the story of a tribal group in New Guinea that was appalled when the American anthropologist living in their midst allowed her newborn infant to cry without immediately picking the baby up. The American mother was merely adhering to a cultural belief about parenting. The indigenous New Guinea group was concerned that if the baby cried too long, its spirit would escape through the open fontanel, leading to the child's death.

Although much of the violence in our society occurs in families, violence can also be institutionalized, as in schools that allow corporal punishment of children. Many parents, teachers, and administrators argue in favor of corporal punishment in schools, pointing out that banning corporal punishment would remove from teachers the power to control students. This argument ignores the fact that there are more effective techniques for responding to misbehavior and for maintaining discipline, including encouragement and the use of praise, consistency in the application of rules, recognizing academic weaknesses in particular students and providing specialized help, having high teacher–pupil ratios, and encouraging self-esteem in students. Adults do not like to be hit in public and our society does not condone the use of physical means by adults to settle their differences. Instead, adults thrive on praise and positive reinforcement. These principles also hold true for children.

The American Academy of Pediatrics believes that "corporal punishment may affect adversely a student's self-image and his or her school achievement and that it may contribute to disruptive and violent student behavior" (American Academy of Pediatrics, 1991). In its 1991 statement on Corporal Punishment in Schools, the Academy urges "parents, educators, school administrators, school board members, legislators and other adults to seek (1) the legal prohibition by all states of corporal punishment in schools and (2) the employment of alternative methods of managing student behavior" (p. 173).

An international perspective supports the view that corporal punishment can be eliminated in schools without affecting quality education. In many countries, corporal punishment has not been allowed in schools for several generations, and the fabric of their societies has not disintegrated. For example, corporal punishment in schools was abolished in the Netherlands (1820), Italy (1860), Belgium (1867), France (1881), Finland (1890), Norway (1936), Sweden (1958), Switzerland (1970), and England (1986).

Children learn far more at school than the basics of reading, writing, and mathematics. They learn how to relate to others and how to solve problems in human relationships from the day-to-day examples given by their teachers. Hitting children in school may teach them that conflicts can, and perhaps should, be resolved by violence, a lesson that may bear fruit in the adult and parenting relationships many of these children will ultimately have.

The perceptive reader will have realized that this last sentence could give a simplistic view of child abuse, suggesting that it is a learned behavior. Certainly, childhood experiences may contribute to abusive behavior in adult life. However, there are a number of other models that have been used to explain child physical abuse. A brief review of some of these models will be the basis for an attempt to then take a broader view as to the causes of physical abuse. Models that have been used to explain physical abuse can be looked at under two broad headings—societal factors and family factors—with family factors being further broken down into adult factors and child factors.

SOCIETAL FACTORS

Stress and Socioeconomic Factors

One view contends that a fundamental problem in regard to child abuse is a social structure that condones poverty and physical force in child rearing. This argument suggests that the origins of personal violence can be found in the violence seen in society, which is often institutionalized by society. The family is merely a microcosm of society, reflecting what is bad as well as what is good in the society in which it functions. It is known that stress and the problems of drugs and alcohol are associated with child abuse. Stressful events have been shown to have a direct relationship with child abuse. The greater the number of stressful events in parents' lives, the higher is the incidence of child abuse, while parents who experience the least stress have the lowest rate of child abuse (Straus et al., 1980). Forty-one percent of families with alcohol or drug addiction have been shown to have abused or neglected their children (Black & Mayer, 1980), although this high incidence is not consistent across all studies.

While it is important to stress that child physical abuse and neglect occur across the entire social spectrum, the reality is that a disproportionate number of cases are found in families in poor socioeconomic circumstances. Economic factors, interpersonal relations, and sociocultural relations act together in these families to create severe economic stress and hardship. Some authors have claimed that this is the single greatest threat to family functioning.

Child physical abuse can be linked with other violent and criminal behavior. For example, figures from the United Kingdom (Creighton & Noyes, 1989) show that 15% of mothers and 41% of fathers had criminal records before the case of abuse was diagnosed. Violent offenses were overrepresented among these crimes compared with the incidence of violent offenses for crimes on a national basis. The physical abuse of children by fathers had its strongest link with fathers who had been convicted of violent crimes against other adults.

FAMILY FACTORS AND ADULT CHARACTERISTICS

The Parents

Psychoanalytic View

In this view, the primary cause of child abuse is seen to be the parents' own psychological problems. The parents are seen as often having been abused in their own childhood and thus having learned to use abuse as a disciplinary technique. Their basic needs to be loved, to be dependent, and to be nurtured as children were never adequately met and so they unrealistically look to their own children to meet these needs. They have high standards for and unrealistic expectations of their children, expecting them to understand their needs and to provide the nurturing they missed out on in their own childhood—the concept of "role reversal." In addition, these parents are often so concerned with their own needs that they are unable to understand and meet the needs of their own children. Sometimes, a supportive partner can provide the parent with the support that is needed, but often both parents come from similar backgrounds and so are unable to support each other.

As a result of their childhood experiences, they do not develop the concept of basic trust. Thus, in their adult lives they have few close friends, with very little in the way of social networks, and they are unable to use the family, friends, and community resources that most parents utilize to cope with some of the day-to-day stresses of child rearing.

The psychoanalytic view is an important one that does explain many of the characteristics found in abusive parents. However, it does not explain the whole problem, not accounting for the fact that the majority of abusive parents were not abused as children and not accounting for the sociological factors that interact with these psychological factors in helping to determine whether abuse will occur. By assuming that the entire cause of the problem lies with the adult, there is the danger of overlooking other contributing factors, such as complexity of family function, factors in the child, and outside stresses and influences.

Learned Behavior

It is believed that many of our parenting skills are largely determined in childhood. If children learn that violence is an acceptable part of family life, they may incorporate this value into their own behavior. For example, Straus and Kantor (1987) showed that child abuse rates are significantly higher in families whose parents identified their own fathers as having hit their mothers.

Attachment Theory

Bowlby (1969) proposed that the survival of humans, particularly the human infant, depends to some extent on having an attachment figure, usually a parent. The infant elicits responses from the parent, which draw the two together. The process of attachment develops in the early months and years of life. It is closely linked with the behavior and responsiveness of the mother. If the mother, or other caregiver, is unresponsive to the infant or is inaccessible or responds inappropriately, then the child is likely to become anxious and insecure in its attachment. Some maltreated children have been shown to have problems in their attachment, particularly in the level of anxiety associated with the attachment to their parent.

People who have insecure attachment relationships from their childhood tend to be less flexible and less resourceful, more anxious and more hostile. They tend to be lonelier and to have less supportive peer and family relationships. Attachment experiences in early life do seem to have considerable influence on the quality of the interpersonal relationships that are established in later childhood and in adult life. This has implications for the way in which adults are able to relate to their own children.

Intergenerational Transmission

Intergenerational transmission suggests that abused children will themselves become abusive parents. This is true in some cases, but not in the majority. Kaufman and Zigler (1987) found that there was little objective evidence for the intergenerational view. According to the evidence that was available, approximately 30% of adults who were abused as children abuse their own children. From the other point of view, when looking at parents who have abused their children, one sees many who were not abused in their own childhood. Although there is a link, it is important for professionals, parents, and the public to realize that the cycle is not inevitable and that in most cases it will not be repeated. However, this does not mean that appropriate treatment for abused children is not required to reduce the strength of this link. Clearly, there will be ameliorating factors, such as other supportive relationships, that will reduce the likelihood that the abuse will be repeated in the next generation.

Parent Factors

In addition to their own child-rearing experiences, a number of characteristics have been described as more common in physically abusive parents. These include a rate of depression in abusive mothers double that of mothers of the same socioeconomic class (Kaplan et al., 1983), and low emotional maturity, poor ego strength, and poor mental health (Belsky & Vondra, 1989). Maltreating parents tend to be younger when they have their children (although this is probably confounded by low social class), to be more simplistic and egocentric in their thinking, to have a higher level of poor physical health, and to be less mature in the expression and regulation of their emotions. Low self-esteem and negative affect have also been described. These problems are often associated with poor marital relationships, so that this important source of social support may not be available. Clearly, these factors interact with the other societal factors and the parent's own experiences to lead to a situation where the child's needs for adequate nurturance and protection cannot be met.

The Children

Children born prematurely or following long and difficult labors have been reported as being at increased risk for abuse (Lynch & Roberts, 1977; Jeffcoate, Humphrey, & Lloyd, 1979). This may be so because of interference with attachment, although the great majority of children with these early problems do not become abused. Other factors around the pregnancy may also contribute to the risk of abuse. For example, the pregnancy may be unwanted, or the child may not be of the desired sex. The natural father of the child may not be the mother's spouse. Also, the child may place an increased and unwanted financial burden on the parents, interfere with their previous lifestyle, or disrupt their education and career plans.

There may also be characteristics of the child that increase the risk of abuse. These may include a developmental disability, a physical handicap, a difficult temperament, or an acute or chronic illness. Behavior difficulties in abused children are particularly difficult to sort out as the abusive environment may be an important factor that has led to or exacerbated the behavior disturbances. Abused children have been shown to be regarded by their mothers as being more difficult and more aggressive in play at preschool. However, it is probably meaningless to try to work out how much the child contributes to the abuse. What is important to recognize is that while certain factors in the child over which the child usually has no control may contribute to a situation that precipitates abuse, the abuse cannot be said to be the child's fault.

Child physical abuse is clearly a complex, multidimensional problem. It is not surprising that none of the above factors is in itself a sufficient explanation. It is helpful to think of these as potential risk factors. Abuse is more likely to occur when these factors operate in a cumulative and interactive way. They can influence each other so that abuse may occur when positive support in the family and in the society that reduces the influence of risk factors is not sufficient to overcome the cumulative, interactive effect of these various stresses. As the number of stresses and risk factors increases, the balance changes so that the quality of parenting falls and the risk of abuse rises.

However, even this approach that considers an accumulation and interaction of risk factors in the family and society is insufficient. This is so because our information is based on abusive families who have come to the attention of child protective agencies. We assume, but we do not know, that these families are typical of the larger number of abusive families where abuse goes undetected. It may be that if we had data on the total population of physically abusive families, we would be able to identify additional contributing factors.

SEXUAL ABUSE

Why Are Children Sexually Abused?

Many professionals, especially those who have had children of their own, are able to understand how it could be possible for an adult to suddenly lose control and injure a child. The sudden, impulsive, single episode of physical abuse is not that difficult to comprehend. An appreciation of the stresses associated with child rearing, the condoning of violence by society, and the early childhood experiences of many abusers help professionals to see how physical abuse can be repeated in some families.

However, the same professionals find sexual abuse much more difficult to understand. We may believe that sex is an activity reserved for adults, that children are innocent and should be protected, that only those with the most perverted personality could sexually misuse a child. The truth is different. Sexual abusers are not the stereotype of an unknown stranger in a raincoat standing on a street corner. Sex abusers can be parents, relatives, teachers, doctors, neighbors, child-care workers. In fact, they can come from any field of work and from any social group.

From the point of view of the sexual abuser, the child is an ideal victim. The child knows that responsible adults should be obeyed. The child believes that the threats of the abusing adult may be carried out if the child tells of the abuse, so he or she does not reveal it and then feels confused and guilty. Successful child molesters are often attractive to children and parents and they cultivate these characteristics so that parents are happy for them to mind their children or take them on outings. However, many sexual abusers do not have to cultivate these skills, as the victim is in their own family.

Who Does It?

Most studies suggest that approximately one quarter of cases are the result of stranger abuse, whereas in the other three quarters of cases, the child knows the offender. In approximately half of the cases where the child knows the offender, that person is a member of the child's own family. In the other half, the offender is often a trusted friend who has access to the child.

It is well established that most child molesters are male. Finkelhor and Russell (1984), reviewing evidence about female perpetrators, concluded that sexual abuse by females does occur, with approximately 5% of girls being abused by females, and the incidence rising to 20% for boys. Although their review dispels the view held by some that sexual abuse by females never occurs, it also demonstrates that sexual abuse is primarily committed by males.

Russell (1984) pointed out the particularly high incidence of intrafamilial abuse by stepfathers. In Russell's random sample, one out of every six women who had a stepfather as a principal figure in her childhood years was sexually abused by him. The comparable figure for biological fathers was 1 in 40. The sort of abuse perpetrated by stepfathers was also more severe than that by biological fathers, with 47% of stepfather abuse being classified at the very serious level of violation as compared with 26% for the biological fathers.

How Do They Do It?

Sgroi, Blick, and Porter (1982) described five phases of gradually escalating involvement between the abuser and the child: the engagement phase, the sexually interactive phase, the secrecy phase, the disclosure phase, and a suppressive phase, which sometimes follows disclosure. Although these phases primarily relate to intrafamilial abuse, the same principles hold true for abuse by acquaintances and, in some instances, also for stranger abuse.

In the engagement phase, the perpetrator first has access to the child. This is not difficult if the perpetrator is a family member or a person in a position of trust in whose care the child has been left. The perpetrator then has to work out how to get the child to participate in some sexual behavior without using force and without frightening the child. This is usually done by having the child play a "game" that involves some type of low-grade sexual activity, such as genital exposure. The child may be told that the game is "special" or "a secret." Even though the activity is a misrepresentation of moral standards, the authority of the adult is used to convince the child that the behavior is acceptable. Bribes or other inducements may be offered, although often the authority of the adult, usually an adult whom the child likes, is sufficient.

The engagement phase is followed by a phase of sexual interaction. This may occur on the same day as the engagement phase or on a subsequent occasion. The sexual interaction is usually progressive. It may start as showing the child how to masturbate and then progress to fondling the body in general, going on to focus on the genitals. From fondling, the behavior may lead to a variety of forms of penetration, depending partly on the age of the child. This can include oral sexual activity, digital penetration of the rectum or vagina, or penile penetration. While the type of abuse may vary, the predominant pattern is one of gradually increasing progression of sexual activity.

Secrecy is essential if the adult is not to be detected. Secrecy is part of the engagement and sexual interaction phases. In addition to being essential to avoid detection, it allows these activities to be repeated and perhaps escalated.

There are two main reasons why so many sexually abused children keep it secret. The reason that is easiest to understand is that threats may be used to keep the secret. Young children are relatively powerless and often are not in a position to know whether or not the threats of a seemingly powerful adult will be kept. The threat may be directed against the child: "If you tell anyone, your mommy and daddy will punish you and you will be sent away to live in a home for bad girls." At other times, the threat may be against the child physically: "If you tell anyone, you will be cut open," or the threat may be against someone whom the child loves: "If anyone finds out about this, your mommy will be killed." Threats such as this not only make the child comply with the abuse, but also give the child a feeling of grave responsibility, a feeling that he or she has to keep complying with the perpetrator's demands to keep the family together or to save a loved one from death or injury (Summitt, 1983).

The other reason is more difficult to appreciate. In some instances, the child has kept the secret because some aspects of the activity are enjoyable and the child wants them to continue. The child may enjoy the flattery and gifts from the perpetrator. The child may enjoy the special relationship and the feeling of importance that goes with the activity. This is not to imply that sexual abuse is the child's fault or that the child initiates the sexual behavior. However, it does recognize that these premature sexual experiences can provide the child with gratification at several levels and helps to explain why the sexual abuse may not be revealed.

The phase of secrecy ends when the abuse is discovered. It may be found out by accident, such as when another member of the family walks into a room and observes the abuse. Occasionally, some sexually provocative behavior on the child's part may arouse suspicion. At other times, there may be a physical injury, the appearance of a sexually transmitted disease, or pregnancy. There is also the chance that the child will tell someone the secret, although not necessarily because the child wishes to punish the perpetrator or wishes the abuse to stop. Young children sometimes just want to share the secret and so they tell another child, who then tells an adult. A school protective behaviors program may be the reason why some children disclose. Older children approaching adolescence may change their views about the abuser (in the case of father–daughter abuse, they may start to become more critical of their father) and may want more freedom, something that the abuser resists.

Different families react differently to the disclosure. While some families are supportive of the child, arrange for appropriate professional assessment, and try to protect the child, the reaction in other families may be quite different. The child may be punished for "lying." The family may close ranks in cases of intrafamilial abuse and refuse to believe that such a thing could happen in their family. Even siblings may be angry with the child for disrupting what was outwardly a coherent, respectable family. At times, the pressure is so great that the child reluctantly agrees that the abuse did not happen after all (Summitt, 1983).

Is Child Sexual Abuse on the Rise?

We know that sexual abuse has occurred throughout history. We have enough evidence from surveys to know that it is common today. But is it more common in this generation than in the last or more common than it was several generations ago? One sometimes hears people say that sexual abuse is a direct result of changes in sexual attitudes and behaviors over the last 30 years. The prohibitions against premarital sex and other types of sexual activity are far less strong than they were a generation ago. People whose sexual behavior previously would have been regulated by strong external controls may now be at greater risk of carrying out sexually abusive actions. The availability of pornography, particularly pornography portraying sex with children, may be providing a message that tempts some to follow, perhaps more readily than in the past, as it is indicative of fewer external controls and a more liberal attitude toward sexual activity.

Finkelhor (1984) has suggested that changing expectations by women for sexual satisfaction, making them more critical of male sexual performance, may threaten some men who prefer passive, compliant sexual partners. For such men, a child may be an attractive sexual alternative. Others believe that the widespread increase in divorces, often accompanied by remarriage or common-law marriages, has led to an increase in sexual abuse. There is good evidence that when children live with a stepfather, or with their mother's boyfriend, the risk of sexual abuse is greater than if the partner is the child's natural father (Russell, 1984). However, in other cases, divorce and separation have allowed some children to escape from abusive family members.

While all of these factors may have contributed somewhat to the incidence of child sexual abuse, there is evidence that it has been a common problem for several generations, at least. For example, the 1953 survey by Kinsey et al., where 95% of the female respondents were born before 1929, showed a prevalence of 24% preadolescent sexual abuse. Leventhal (1990) has suggested comparing the rates of reported abuse between older adults and younger adults who participated in the same survey. This approach has the advantage that the same methodology was used to obtain data from the younger and older adults. A review of seven population-based studies where ages of respondents are available showed that in five studies the older subjects gave a history of sexual abuse less frequently than did the younger ones (Leventhal, 1990), although memory impairment in older subjects may be a potential problem in this type of comparison.

The information so far tells us a number of facts about child sexual abuse, but still does not answer the question of why some adults sexually abuse children.

Risk Factors

Our knowledge of the victims of child sexual abuse has shown that some children are at greater risk than others. For a start, girls are at a greater risk than boys. Some of the other risk factors are a little harder to be certain of, be-cause some characteristics may be a result of the abusive experience rather than factors that increase the risk of the abuse.

These factors have been reviewed by Finkelhor and Baron (1986). While the studies consistently point out that belonging to any one social class or ethnic group is not a risk factor for sexual abuse (sexual abuse is distributed reasonably evenly across the social spectrum), certain features are more common. The most constant finding in studies shows that, apart from female sex, the preadolescent age group is a time of greater risk than younger or older age groups. Parental absence and unavailability seem to increase the risk of sexual abuse. Victims of child sexual abuse are more likely to have lived without the natural father and to have lived with a stepfather or the mother's boyfriend. They are more likely to have mothers who are employed outside the home, or who are ill or disabled. They are more likely to have a poor relationship with one of their parents and to come from homes where they tend to witness conflict between their parents. Abused children have fewer friends in childhood. It is not clear from the studies whether this lack of friends makes them more vulnerable to an abusive adult or whether it is the result of their abusive experiences.

Abusers

It would be nice if a single theory could explain why people sexually abuse children. Unfortunately, no single theory explains the whole problem. There are several theories that describe some aspects of why child sexual abuse occurs, but it would be simplistic to think that such a complex problem could be explained by a single-factor theory. We know a number of things about abusers, but none by itself is sufficient to explain all abuse. For example, one simple and incorrect view is that all child sexual abusers were themselves victims of child sexual abuse. The evidence suggests that a large proportion of sexual abusers were *not* molested during their own childhood. Many of the abused do not become abusers. If being abused were the only factor that led to someone's becoming an abuser, then, as most abused children are female, it would follow that most abusers would also be female. This is clearly not the case. A major criticism of the view that being abused leads to becoming an abuser is that not only is this view correct in only some of cases, but victims of child sexual abuse and their parents, when they hear this view, naturally fear that they will become abusers. Apart from the serious anxiety this causes, in some instances the expectation may lead to a self-fulfilling prophecy.

Other factors observed in sexually abusive adults are more common in sexual abusers, but are not prerequisites for abuse and are not necessarily conditions leading to abuse. These include the view that abusers are arrested in their psychosexual development and thus relate more readily to children in social relationships. Their low self-esteem makes it easier for them to feel powerful and in control when they are interacting with children. Some have suggested that abusers attempt to overcome the sense of powerlessness they experienced during some severe childhood trauma by having power and control over a child. Another view is that some who have had early childhood sexual experiences still find children sexually arousing in adult life, finding that children are easier to relate to sexually than adults. Pornography may be used to assist this sexual arousal, as may drugs and alcohol.

All of these factors add to knowledge about sexual abusers, but give only part of the picture. A valuable contribution to understanding why some adults sexually abuse children has been provided by Finkelhor (1984), who describes a model in which four preconditions need to be met before sexual abuse occurs:

1. The adult must have sexual feelings for the child or for children in general.
2. The adult most overcome his or her internal in-hibitions against acting out the sexual feeling.
3. The adult must overcome the external obstacles to acting out the sexual feeling.
4. The adult must overcome resistance or attempts at avoidance by the child.

The first precondition is a motivation to sexually abuse. Finkelhor believes there are three components to this

motivation. First, there needs to be an emotional congru-
ence between the adult and child so that relating sexually
to the child will satisfy some important emotional need for
the adult. These may include a number of factors, such as
arrested emotional development in the adult, the need for
the adult to be powerful and controlling, and a narcissistic
identification where the adult sees himself or herself as a
young child or reenacts a childhood trauma. The second
component of motivation is sexual arousal, where the child
becomes a potential source of sexual satisfaction for the
adult. This may be a result of various factors: a childhood
sexual experience that conditioned the adult, the adult's
misinterpretation of arousal cues from a child, the fact that
the adult becomes stimulated by child pornography, or a
male tendency at times to sexualize emotional needs. The
third component is that alternative sources of sexual gratification are not available for the adult or are less satisfying.
The adult may have a fear of adult females, may have
inadequate social skills, or may have castration anxiety or
an unresolved oedipal conflict.

The second precondition is that the adult has to overcome internal inhibitions against sexual activities with a
child. It is possible that a significant proportion of people
have a strong sexual interest in children, but do not go any
further because of their internal inhibitions. A number of
factors may contribute to the weakening of such internal
inhibitions. These include the use of alcohol or other
drugs, a social toleration of sexual interest in children,
relatively weak criminal sanctions against offenders, and a
social toleration for deviances committed while under the
influence of alcohol.

Finkelhor's third precondition is overcoming external
inhibitors. The potential abuser has external restraints
from a variety of areas, particularly from those who super-
vise and care for the child. Some of these restraints can be
overcome when the person has access to the child, such as
being a member of the child's family or being an adult
who is alone in a position of trust with the child. Factors

that can contribute to overcoming these external factors include a mother who is absent, ill, or not protective of her child; a father who dominates the rest of the family, or unusual sleeping and room-sharing conditions in the family household.

Having the desire to have sexual relationships with a child and having overcome one's own internal inhibitions and the external inhibiting factors, the abuser then has to overcome the resistance of the child. Some children are readier victims than others. A child who feels needy and insecure is likely to be more vulnerable to the approaches of a potential abuser who offers attention and affection. A child who is unsupported in the family or does not have a good relationship with parents may not have anywhere to turn to tell about the abuser's initial approaches. Some children are more likely to be abused because they lack information about how to protect themselves from abuse. Other children are bribed, tricked, and coerced, realizing how powerless they are in such a situation.

Finkelhor believes that all four preconditions must be fulfilled for abuse to occur. At any point along this pathway, the abuse may not eventuate. For example, the adult may lose the opportunity to have access to the child (precondition 3) or the child may resist (precondition 4).

CONCLUSION

It can be seen from this chapter that the causes of child physical and sexual abuse are complex. Understanding them is not merely a matter of academic interest. One needs an ongoing understanding of the factors contributing to abuse in order to be able to provide appropriate prevention and treatment programs. Such understanding will enable us to target preventive programs appropriately and, in treatment, should enable therapists not to treat the child in isolation but to look at all of the various factors that led to a situation where abuse occurred.

3

PHYSICAL ABUSE

Some of the characteristics found in adults who physically abuse their children were documented in the previous chapter. This chapter will focus on the characteristics of abused children, the need to have an awareness of physical abuse as a possibility for a child's injuries, the range of injuries seen in physical abuse; the assessment, investigation, and documentation required when there is a concern about physical abuse.

CHARACTERISTICS OF ABUSED CHILDREN

Children who have been physically abused have been described as having a number of behavioral characteristics. Some of these are a result of the abuse. Others may be predisposing factors that make some children more difficult to manage and so more prone to be abused if they happen to be in a family with a variety of abuse risk factors.

Features Found in Abused Children at the Time of Diagnosis

Physically abused children are often apathetic and withdrawn following the injury. At the same time, they are often visually alert, constantly scanning their environment for signs of danger. This apathy, combined with visual alertness, has been graphically described as "frozen watchfulness" (Ounsted & Lindsay, 1974).

Abused children have also been described as having an impaired self-concept, as having failed to develop basic trust, and as having overall impairment of ego functioning (Green, 1978). They have been described as appearing to be superficially well adjusted but aloof, unable to form meaningful relationships and with a fear of becoming dependent (Yates, 1981). Descriptions such as these come from groups of physically abused children whose injuries have come to the attention of authorities or who have been referred for treatment. Therefore, it cannot be assumed that these characteristics are typical of physically abused children as a whole.

McRae and Longstaffe (1982) classified the wide range of behaviors seen in abused children into four major categories, which could be used to understand the child's needs so that the child could be provided with a specific treatment program based on these needs.

1. Behavior seen as the child's attempt to cope with a hostile environment.
2. Behavior primarily related to emotional abuse, with the physical abuse being a more minor part of the problem.
3. Behavior and development that are normal in spite of the abuse.
4. Behavior that is influenced by the massive nature of the injuries.

This is a useful classification as management of abused children does have to be individually tailored to the child's emotional background, future environment, and needs.

The Way the Parents Perceive the Child

Parents who have abused their children may have perceived the child as being different from the time of birth or even from before birth. In a series of abused children who were compared with their nonabused siblings, Lynch (1976) found that many parents claimed their abused child was different and more difficult to rear than their other children who had not been abused. This finding was confirmed in a much larger sample (Herrenkohl & Herrenkohl, 1979) where parental attitudes toward 295 abused children were studied and compared with the attitudes of these same parents toward the nonabused siblings of the abused children. It was found that, compared with their siblings, the abused children were viewed more negatively by their parents and were often described by them in derogatory terms.

Poor Health and Physical Handicap

While some authorities have reported a higher incidence of congenital abnormalities or chronic illness in abused children, these findings have not been confirmed in all series. Selection bias most likely has been the reason for these differences. It would not be surprising if in families with a predisposition to child abuse the additional stresses caused by having a handicapped child were enough to tip the balance and result in abuse in some cases.

An increased incidence of abuse in twins has been described. It could be argued that a higher incidence of prematurity and other complications among twins may be more important risk factors than simply the presence of having to contend with twins. However, one study (Groothuis et al., 1982) showed that, even when these variables were taken into account, twin status was the most predictive factor of child abuse, suggesting that the increased stress of rearing twins is the extra risk factor.

Although some abused children are described as being withdrawn, with inwardly turned aggressive behavior, such as hair pulling and suicide attempts, most well-controlled studies of young physically abused children show aggressive behavior. A comparison of 20 abused children with 20 nonabused children showed that the abused children were more aggressive in their free play and fantasy play, and also more aggressive on psychological testing, suggesting that children exposed to aggressive parental models are likely to demonstrate aggressive characteristics in situations outside the home (Reidy, 1977). George and Maine (1979) compared a group of abused children in a preschool situation with a control group from families experiencing stress. The abused children were more likely to assault other children at the preschool. They were more verbally aggressive to the staff and less likely to approach the staff in response to friendly overtures. These earlier studies have been supported by a recent study of physically abused children in the 5-to-8-year age range who had more aggressive behavior than did controls (Prino & Peyrot, 1994).

These findings are in contrast to a controlled study by Jacobson and Straker (1982), which did not find increased aggressiveness in the behavior of abused children aged 5 to 10 years, but did show that these children were less socially interactive than their controls.

A problem with studies such as these is that there is often little or no information about the interval between the abuse and the behavioral assessment or about whether or not the children had been in treatment. This makes it difficult to know whether the described behaviors are a result of the physical abuse, or of remaining in the disturbed environment that led to the abuse or whether the behaviors have been improved and modified by any intervention that may have been given.

The Contribution of the Child

To simply look at the child as a passive recipient of abuse ignores the importance of the interaction between the parent and the child and the likelihood that some children, by their behavior, may precipitate an abusive incident in a predisposed parent. In parents where there is the potential for abuse, it is possible that some aspect of the child, such as delayed development or provocative behavior, may be enough to precipitate an abusive incident.

Abused children, when observed with their parents in a structured laboratory setting and when compared with normal children, have been found to relate to their parents in ways that caused feelings of inadequacy in the mothers about not being able to meet their children's needs. Their behaviors also caused feelings of rage in the mothers about their child's demanding attitude (Gaensbauer & Sands, 1970).

The view that child abuse is exclusively a function of problems in the parents and problems in society is a little too simple. Certain children produce particular parental stress reactions, and some of these reactions may precipitate abuse in predisposed parents. Such characteristics may include infant temperament, developmental delay, constant and unusual crying patterns, and other personality characteristics.

The wide range of behavior seen in abused children suggests that there is no such thing as a typical abused child. In addition to the way in which parents perceive undesirable features in these children, the child's own behavior may contribute to or precipitate the abuse. While it is not the fault of the child that abuse occurs, it can be seen that characteristics of some children will make them more prone to abuse, when in a risk situation, than others. It is also of concern that the aggressive and withdrawn behavior shown by many abused children is likely to have important implications for the way they develop relationships in their adult lives.

AN AWARENESS OF CHILD PHYSICAL ABUSE

It is still not unusual for there to be denial that abuse may be the explanation for some injuries to children. While it is the abusive parents who are most active in denying the true cause of the injury, others, including family members and friends of the family, as well as professionals, may also deny the problem. Denial is best seen as a coping mechanism to reduce the stress that occurs when the diagnosis of abuse is raised. The problem with denial is that it can prevent effective intervention and protection for the child.

Denial can be a problem for doctors: many older doctors are poorly trained in dealing with abuse; some may be reluctant to become involved in something that is likely to lead to court; and others may be uncomfortable working cooperatively with other professionals, something that is usually required for the effective management of physical abuse.

Sometimes, the doctor, whose professional rewards usually come from the gratitude of a family who have been successfully treated, can feel very uncomfortable when confronted with an abused child and the parents. There may be a temptation to accept at face value a most unlikely explanation for an injury rather than to seek out its real cause. On the other hand, professionals can be overzealous in diagnosing child abuse, finding it when it has not occurred. Children suffer bruises in normal play, so that clearly every bruise is not due to child abuse even though an overenthusiastic neighbor, day-care worker, or health and welfare professional may overinterpret such signs. Similarly, the pigmented marks ("Mongolian spots") often seen on the backs of children of African and Asian background are sometimes falsely attributed to child abuse by inexperienced or overenthusiastic personnel. The diagnosis of physical abuse is a fine balance between denial and overinterpretation, although the problem of denial is usually far greater. It is important to look at each case with an open mind, with no preconceived ideas, taking a thoroughly professional approach and seeking expert assistance when uncertain.

Even before the injury is seen, there are clues in the presentation that alert one to the possibility of physical abuse. Following the injury, the parents may take the child to a hospital, doctor, or health care center for treatment. The most important question that should be asked is, "Is the history given to explain the injuries consistent with the findings?"

Jennifer, aged 2 months, was brought to the hospital because of a painful, swollen upper leg. Her mother said that Jennifer had been placed on the couch, but that when she temporarily left the room Jennifer must have accidentally rolled off the couch onto the floor, where she was lying when the mother reentered the room. Jennifer was found to have extensive bruising on one side of the skull. An x-ray showed a skull fracture as well as a spiral fracture of the femur. In addition, the x-rays showed some healing rib fractures that had clearly occurred at an earlier time.

The injuries and the mother's story are inconsistent. Two-month-olds are not able to roll, so there is no reason why Jennifer should have fallen from the couch. Even if Jennifer had been able to roll, the spiral fracture of the femur would be unusual in a simple fall and would be more likely caused by a twisting injury of the limb. The old rib fractures showed that there had been a previous significant injury. In addition, a skull fracture with extensive bruising is very unlikely when falling from a couch onto a carpeted floor. A review of 207 cases where children fell from beds found only one simple skull fracture and one broken clavicle. There were no serious or multiple injuries (Lyons & Oates, 1993).

When looking at the injury, the physician should ask, "Could these injuries have occurred in the way they are said to have occurred?" It may be found that the injuries are too severe, too many, of the wrong type, and in the wrong distribution.

There are certain patterns of injury that strongly suggest abuse. These include bruises in a young baby (young babies should not become bruised during normal care), multiple or severe injuries following a fall from a short distance or while running, fractures in children in the first year of life, rib fractures, signs of raised pressure within the brain and retinal hemorrhages in an infant (usually the result of violent shaking), and multiple small burns that could be consistent with cigarette burns.

In addition, there may be a story of frequent previous injuries, some of which may be of a suspicious nature and where the parents, possibly to avoid detection, had taken the child to a different health facility on each occasion. Sometimes, the behavior of the parents is unusual. They may delay bringing the child for medical advice. They may be indifferent to the severity of the child's injuries. They may become aggressive, refusing proper investigation and treatment, and at times they may give conflicting or even vague explanations for the child's injury.

An unreasonable time delay between the occurrence of the injury and the parents' bringing the child for medical help is a warning sign, especially if the injury is severe. For example, the infant may have had a serious head injury leading to loss of consciousness, but be left in the crib by the parents for several hours and brought for medical attention only if there was deterioration, such as gasping respirations or seizures.

TYPES OF INJURIES

Bruises and Other Superficial Injuries

Bruises are common in children and are often due to genuine, usually minor, accidents. Children tend to run into objects, sustaining bruises on the forward-facing body surfaces. Bruises on the forehead, above the eye, around the nose, and on the shins, knees, and elbows are common and usually accidental. What makes one suspicious that bruising may be from abuse is its pattern and distribution.

Bruises are the most common feature of physical abuse, being seen in approximately 90% of abused children.

Bruises may show a pattern of adult fingers where the child has been firmly grasped. These may be seen on the face, where there may be a thumbprint on one cheek and several fingerprints on the other cheek, or over the chest and abdomen. Bruises on the thighs, buttocks, and lower back are often a result of severe punishment. Bruises and abrasions around the face and head are common when a child is hit or slapped. The external ear may show bruising where the child has been hit on the side of the head and where the ear is compressed between the adult's hand or fist and the bone of the skull.

Injuries to the lower jaws and upper lip may occur during attempts at forced feeding or as a result of the parent's losing control when the child refuses to eat. Bruises and injuries around the lower abdomen or inner aspects of the thighs should raise the question of whether there has also been sexual abuse.

Although black eyes can occur accidentally, their presence should raise the question of child abuse, especially if both eyes are involved.

Sometimes, the bruises show a pattern. In addition to the pattern of fingerprints already mentioned, there may be handprints from slaps, linear marks where the child has been hit with a hard object, loop marks from a coil of rope or electrical cord, and marks left by a strap, where occasionally the imprint of a buckle is seen.

More unusual marks occur when a child is pushed against a patterned object, such as the imprint of a carpet or a carpet burn where the child's body skids along the carpet. Human bites show a pair of crescent-shaped bruise patterns. These are different from animal bites, which result in puncture wounds.

Children who have been injured on more than one occasion will show bruises of different ages. Bruises change color over time, although there is some variation so that it is difficult to be precise about the age of a bruise. Table 1 is an aid to assessing the age of the bruise. It can be seen that there is some overlap in the ages of the bruises, reflecting the lack of precision in this area.

Table 1

Age of Bruise	Color
Up to 2 days	Reddish, purple, swollen and tender
2 to 5 days	Red, blue, purple, brownish
4 to 7 days	Brownish-green
7 to 10 days	Yellow
Over 10 days	Brown
14 to 24 days	Cleared

Burns

About 10% of physical abuse cases are burns, with hot-water burns the most common. A common scenario is for a parent to dunk the child's buttocks into boiling water as a punishment for soiling. This leaves a distinctive burn pattern involving the cheeks of both buttocks.

Gloria, age 18 months, was brought to the emergency room of a hospital with burns on both buttocks. Her mother said that she had been running the bath for Gloria, that the water must have been too hot, and when she was momentarily distracted by the telephone, Gloria must have attempted to get into the bath herself, sustaining the burns. The physical examination revealed burns on the buttocks but nowhere else. As it is not possible for a child to place only her buttocks in the bath, the only explanation could be that she was held in the hot water by an adult.

Burns that have a circumferential glove or stocking distribution (i.e., covering the hands and forearms or feet and lower legs) should raise a suspicion that the child has been forcibly held in hot water. Other deliberate burns may also leave a pattern. The most common is the cigarette burn, which may leave multiple marks. Other patterns may be seen when the child is held against a hot object, such as the grill of a radiator or an iron.

It takes only a short time to cause a serious burn. The three factors involved are the temperature, the duration of exposure, and the skin thickness. Mortiz and Henriques (1947), studying adults (whose skin would be thicker than that of children), found that water at 150°F (65°C) took an average of only 1.5 seconds to cause a second-degree burn. At 140°F (60°C), 5 seconds were required, rising to 30 seconds at 130°F and 5 minutes at 120°F.

Abdominal Injuries

Abdominal injuries are usually serious and may be fatal. They are generally the result of a child being kicked, punched, or jumped on. The solid organs within the abdomen, major intraabdominal blood vessels, and the intestine may be torn, resulting in bleeding or peritonitis. Abdominal injury may occur in the presence of other injuries, such as fractures or head injuries. As the abdominal injuries may leave little in the way of external bruising, the doctor's attention may focus on other injuries with obvious signs so that there may be a delay in realizing that there is also a serious, relatively silent, abdominal injury. There is sometimes a silent period of several hours after the abdominal injury, when the child may be relatively quiet or appear to be asleep, before features suggesting a serious problem within the abdomen become apparent.

Eleven-month-old Gary had been well during the day but woke at night crying. This pattern of nighttime waking and crying had been present for several weeks and was causing considerable stress in the family. His father went to his room during the crying episode and after about 10 minutes of his trying to comfort the child, during which time the crying seemed to become worse, the crying suddenly stopped and Gary appeared to go back to sleep. The next day he was pale and difficult to arouse. His respirations were gasping. He was taken to a hospital, but was unable to be resuscitated. An autopsy showed a ruptured liver and intestinal bruising, most likely caused by a direct, powerful blow to the abdomen.

Injuries to the Brain and Eyes

Violent shaking of babies and infants, where the head is relatively large and the neck muscles relatively weak, can cause serious injury within the brain. The repeated acceleration–deceleration and rotation forces caused by shaking can rupture the small blood vessels that run over the surface of the brain, leading to a subdural hematoma. Violent shaking can also cause the brain to be damaged from bumping against the inside of the skull and can damage blood vessels within the substance of the brain, leading to intracranial hemorrhage. Shaking injuries are sometimes, but not always, accompanied by direct head injury. Grab marks where the infant has been held to be shaken may be seen. A shaking injury should always be considered as one of the possibilities in an infant who presents to the emergency room unconscious or with signs of raised intracranial pressure.

Attempts to choke a child can result in asphyxia, where the supply of oxygen to the brain is impaired. This can also cause swelling of the brain and loss of consciousness. Sometimes bruises or petechiae (small, reddish-purple spots where blood has leaked out of damaged blood vessels) are seen around the neck.

Hemorrhages involving the retina of the eye are commonly seen as a result of violent shaking. Other eye injuries can include direct trauma to the tissues around the eye (periorbital hematoma or "black eye") and injuries to the conjunctiva, lens, and cornea, often from a direct attack or penetrating injury to the eye.

Fractures and Other Bone Injuries

Many fractures in children are the result of genuine accidents. For these, there is usually a clear history, a prompt presentation for medical attention, and physical findings, such as fracture type, that are consistent with the story. In accidental fractures, there is usually immediate loss of function of the affected limb due to the pain, while bruising is usually minimal. In abuse, there may be a vague or unlikely explanation for the fracture. There may be excessive bruising around the fracture or suspicious bruising in other areas of the body. A delay in seeking medical attention is sometimes seen. Fractures occurring in the first year of life, particularly in the first 6 months, where children rarely have the ability to get into a position where they can sustain an accidental fracture, should be treated with suspicion and appropriately assessed.

Some important patterns have been described in fractures caused by physical abuse (Hobbs, 1993).

1. *A single fracture with multiple bruises.* Multiple bruising is unusual with a single fracture, suggesting a pulling, grabbing episode that may have led to the fracture.

2. *Multiple fractures in different stages of healing.* In these cases, there may be some bruising or soft tissue injury. Clearly, more than one fracture, with fractures being of different ages, suggests serious injury on more than one occasion. Often the parents are unable to give an explanation for the older fractures.

3. *Metaphyseal-epiphyeal injuries.* These are fractures near the growing ends of the bone. They are

typical child abuse fractures that occur when a limb is pulled or twisted. The relatively weak metaphyseal area of the bone becomes disrupted and this can be seen radiologically. Sometimes, fragments of bone become separated from the ends of the bone. These fractures cause little pain or swelling and so are usually detected only when radiological studies are done because of a concern about physical abuse. The usual areas for metaphyseal fractures are the wrist, elbow, knee, and ankle.

4. *Rib fractures.* These are usually multiple. They probably occur when the infant or child's chest is compressed during a shaking episode or from kicks and blows to the chest. They are often symptomless and detected only when radiological studies are done because of concern about child abuse.

5. *The formation of new periosteal bone.* When the long bone of an infant is injured, there is often a subperiosteal hemorrhage (i.e., bleeding between the membrane that lines the bone [the periosteum] and the bone itself). This bleeding lifts the periosteum from the shaft of the bone and new bone starts to be laid down about 10 to 14 days later. Periosteal elevation and bleeding are usually the result of injuries where the limb is twisted or pulled.

6. *A skull fracture in association with intracranial injuries.* Most skull fractures due to simple falls are not associated with underlying brain injury. Hobbs (1984), in a comparison of skull fractures secondary to child abuse with accidental skull fractures, showed that fractures in abused children were more likely to be multiple or complex, to have associated intracranial injury, to be wide (in contrast to the hairline cracks usually seen in

simple, accidental skull fractures), and to involve more than one of the cranial bones.

The type of fracture is also helpful as certain fractures are more common in abuse. For example, a twisting, shearing force to a child's bone (such as the femur or humerus) will cause a spiral fracture, with the fracture line running along the shaft of the long bone in a spiral fashion.

Janine, who was 8 months old, was brought by her parents to a doctor because they said she cried every time her diaper was changed. Some bruising was noted on the upper aspect of the right thigh. Swelling was also present and movement of the right leg caused discomfort. An x-ray showed a spiral fracture of the right femur. In view of this finding, a radiological study of the whole skeleton was done. This showed several healing rib fractures, several weeks old. The parents were unable to explain any of these injuries, although later Janine's mother said that two days previously, when Janine was screaming during a diaper change, she became frustrated, twisted Janine's upper leg, and heard a cracking sound.

Drowning

Drowning or attempted drowning is a form of child abuse that may be particularly difficult to recognize as it leaves no specific signs. It is important to consider intentional drowning when looking at immersion incidents that are atypical or where the history is vague or conflicting. Although this is a delicate situation, if there is a suspicion of child abuse, careful examination of the body for other injuries and radiological studies to see if there are recent or old unexplained fractures may help to clarify the issue. Feldman (1993), in a review of 95 drownings and near drownings in children, found that only a small number required referral to child protective services and that most of these referrals were for neglect. Intentional immersion may be apparent only after a more thorough evaluation.

Poisoning

Accidental poisoning is a common childhood problem, particularly in toddlers. Sometimes, these episodes of poisoning are due to neglect, where the parent has failed to keep a poisonous substance (such as prescribed medication, petroleum products, and cleaning agents) in a place inaccessible to the child. Few would argue that this is child abuse. However, a small proportion of poisonings are not accidental. The poisonings may be with medication such as tranquilizers, or more often a common household substance is used as a form of punishment. Examples are the child who is forced to eat a large amount of red peppers as a form of punishment, a child who is forced to eat salt, or a child who is forced to drink large amounts of water. Sometimes, poisoning is chronic and repetitive in nature, merging with Munchausen Syndrome by proxy (Factitious Disorder by proxy in DSM-IV). (See page 60.)

Injuries to the Fetus

The fetus is vulnerable to a number of influences, some of which are external but most of which are related to the mother's lifestyle. The most obvious external abuse is physical violence of the mother and fetus. This may result in miscarriage or fetal injury. A more common problem is the effect of tobacco, alcohol, or drugs on the developing fetus. This leads to the complex issue of defining fetal abuse. Cigarette smoking is common during pregnancy. There is good evidence that it causes growth retardation in the fetus, resulting in low birthweight. There is also some evidence of subsequent reading impairment in children whose mothers smoked tobacco during pregnancy.

Excessive alcohol consumption in early pregnancy can lead to the fetal alcohol syndrome. The situation is not clear-cut since the effects on the fetus are variable. The concurrent use of tobacco with poor maternal nutrition complicates the issue further. Children with fetal alcohol syndrome have a variety of problems, including growth deficiency, microcephaly, learning disorders, typical facial features (flat midface; narrow upper lip; thin, indistinct philtrum; and short, upturned nose), and occasional congenital abnormalities. The growth failure and learning problems are permanent and are often accompanied by hyperactivity, impulsivity, and antisocial behavior (Bays, 1990).

Heroin abuse, as well as increasing the risk of abortion, congenital malformations, growth retardation, and neonatal heroin withdrawal, also carries with it the risk of the mother's becoming infected with HIV from using contaminated needles and passing this infection on to the fetus. Cocaine causes spontaneous abortion in approximately 30% of affected pregnancies and increases the risk of placental abruption and hemorrhage 10-fold. In addition, cocaine can cause congenital anomalies, such as microcephaly and delayed, long-lasting withdrawal symptoms. Up to 15% of affected babies are thought to succumb to the sudden infant death syndrome (Bays, 1990).

The area of fetal abuse is complex, although opinion is now moving in the direction of the need for the fetus to be protected from behaviors and substances that are likely to have a deleterious affect on fetal development and on that child's subsequent life.

Child Death and Child Abuse

When a child is found dead or is dead on arrival at a hospital, the cause of death has to be determined. In many cases, the cause of death is obvious. But in other cases, child abuse should be considered as one of the possibilities. In particular, multiple injuries leading to death, said to have resulted from a short fall, should be regarded as suspicious (Lyons & Oates, 1993). Sudden infant death syndrome is the most common cause of sudden death in infancy. Sometimes, a thorough autopsy will show that what initially was labeled as sudden infant death syndrome has had a more sinister underlying cause, such as when intracranial injury or rib fracture is found. Suffocation is difficult to detect and may masquerade as sudden infant death syndrome. Deliberate drowning can also be presented as an accident. Cases of sudden infant death syndrome obviously need to be handled with compassion and sensitivity, as in the great majority of these cases the parents are not to blame. However, a careful autopsy, performed by a pathologist with experience in pediatrics and forensic pathology, is needed to help rule out a nonaccidental cause.

In a review of fatal child abuse cases, it was found that more than half of the children were less than 12 months old. Seventy percent of the deaths were from head injuries, with the remainder resulting from asphyxia or strangulation. Thirty-five percent had evidence of previous physical abuse, suggesting that earlier detection and intervention would have prevented some of these deaths (DeSilva & Oates, 1993).

The increasing number of child death review panels in the United States (Durfee, 1989; Colorado Child Fatality Review Committee, 1990) has led to increased emphasis on reviewing all child deaths. While this has detected a number of fatal child abuse cases that otherwise would have been undetected, such panels have a broader public health aspect in highlighting situations, usually accidental, but occasionally due to medical factors, that led to the child's death so that preventive strategies can be instituted.

Factitious Disorder by Proxy

The term "Munchausen syndrome by proxy"—now Factitious Disorder by proxy (DSM-IV)—was first used to describe children whose mothers invented stories of illness about their child and who fabricated false physical signs in their children to try to substantiate these stories (Meadow, 1977). Rosenberg (1987) reviewed the literature of this condition and suggested that such a diagnosis should have the following characteristics:

1. The illness in the child is fictitious or is an illness that is produced by the child's parent or caregiver.

2. The child is persistently presented to medical professionals for assessment of the symptoms. This usually results in multiple medical procedures and multiple medical opinions.

3. The perpetrator denies knowledge of the cause of the child's illness.

4. When the perpetrator and the child are separated, the acute symptoms and signs abate, although there may be some sequelae, either as a result of what the perpetrator has done to the child or as a result of medical interventions.

Boys and girls are equally affected; the average age of diagnosis is around 3 years, with the "illness" having been present for an average of 14 months before the true cause is discovered (Rosenberg, 1987).

The typical clinical presentations and their causes are shown in Table 2.

The mother at times may coach the child to lie about the symptoms, although usually the child is too young to do so. The symptoms result in hospital admissions and, often, invasive investigations. When simple investigations reveal no cause for the symptoms and as the symptoms persist, investigations become more complex and invasive. Symptoms persist while the child is in the hospital and the mother is seen as being attentive and dedicated. She spends most of her time at the child's bedside and helps the nursing staff in aspects of the treatment.

At 14 months of age, Sally was referred from a peripheral hospital to a university hospital for investigation of persistent fevers. Blood cultures had shown a variety of infectious organisms and she had been treated extensively with a range of intravenous antibiotics. Her mother, who had partially completed nursing training, was attentive and spent much of her time at the bedside. Intravenous access had become

Table 2

Symptom	Cause
Seizures	Made up by mother and never seen by professionals; induced by partial suffocation or partial strangulation.
Apnea	Partial suffocation.
Bleeding (hematemesis, hematuria, rectal, vaginal or nose bleeding)	Blood from another person, usually the mother, is smeared near the appropriate orifice or mixed with urine or feces. Mother's menstrual blood is often used. Occasionally red coloring agents are used.
Diarrhea	Laxative abuse.
Fevers	Injecting contaminated substances into the intravenous line, warming the thermometer, changing the temperature chart.
Rashes/hair loss	Bizarre skin lesions produced by scratching or rubbing; hair pulling or cutting.
Failure to thrive	Food deprivation.
Vomiting	Giving emetics or inducing vomiting mechanically.

difficult in Sally and a small surgical procedure was required to maintain the intravenous route. In the university hospital, the fevers persisted and the child's condition deteriorated. A fungal infection appeared in the bloodstream, possibly secondary to the extensive range of antibiotics that had been used. The organisms grown on culture from the blood were unusual, suggesting that the bloodstream may have been contaminated with feces.

During an infrequent absence by the mother, one of the nursing staff looked into the mother's bag, which had been left in the child's bedside locker. Several syringes were found, containing fluid contaminated with feces. It was felt that the mother had been injecting this material directly into her daughter's intravenous line whenever she took Sally to the bathroom. Maternal access to the child was stopped. Sally's symptoms rapidly subsided. Her mother, even when faced with the evidence, denied any knowledge of interference.

In most cases, the mother tends to be the person who fabricates the illness. The father, often passive and unsupportive, is usually not aware of what is happening. These mothers often have a history of factitious illness or Somatoform Disorder, with Histrionic and Borderline Personality Disorder being a common feature (Bools, Neale, & Meadow, 1994).

The consequences for the children can be serious. They are subjected to frequent hospital admissions and uncomfortable, invasive investigations. They may at times undergo surgery. There is a danger of death or brain damage, especially in cases where the mother has been inducing seizures by smothering if she misjudges the time required to produce the symptoms. There is also a danger of developing "sickness behavior" and invalidism if the child believes he or she is genuinely sick.

The warning signs of Factitious Disorder by proxy include a discrepancy between the child's apparent good health and the symptoms (such as bleeding); an overly attentive mother who appears surprisingly cheerful despite the apparent seriousness of the child's illness; signs and symptoms that become less or absent when the mother is not present; the lack of effective treatment and a history of repeated medical opinions for the symptoms (Wissow, 1990).

In this discussion of the injuries of physical abuse, it is important to stress that the injury is merely an outward physical sign pointing to the need to assess the family. It is often only after such an assessment that one can develop some confidence as to whether or not the injury was nonaccidental. The assessment, which should include an assessment of the family's strengths as well as weaknesses, will give an indication of the subsequent risk to the child and should be the beginning of creating a plan to protect the child. In most cases, the aim should not be to decide how to punish the offender, but to assess the safety of the child's environment, to provide the basis for a treatment plan to improve the parenting skills of the child's parents, and to develop the child's potential for normal development.

AN APPROACH TO ASSESSMENT
IN PHYSICAL ABUSE

The assessment will involve the child, the family, and the environment, including medical, social, and psychological characteristics.

Assessment of the Child

Physical Assessment

It is important for the whole child to be thoroughly examined. A helpful factor in making the diagnosis of physical abuse is the presence of multiple injuries or unexplained injuries at different stages of healing, and such evidence should be carefully sought. Injuries should be documented precisely and legibly, for example, by giving the size, color, and location of bruises. Photographs of the injuries should be taken.

The medical investigations required are minimal. If there is bruising, coagulation studies should be done to rule out an underlying bleeding disorder. Bleeding disorders are rarely confused with physical abuse and are much more uncommon, so the results will usually be negative. However, it is useful to exclude a bleeding disorder as this may be raised by the family or in court as a possible explanation for the child's bruises.

Radiological studies can be valuable. In addition to a radiograph of areas where a fracture may be suspected, a skeletal survey, looking for other or old fractures at different stages of healing, should be considered and probably should be done routinely in children two years of age or less. As periosteal elevation will not show on a radiograph in its initial stages, a radionuclide scan, where areas of periosteal elevation will show as "hot spots," may also provide valuable data. It is important for the assessment to be done by an experienced pediatrician as occasionally rare conditions, such as osteogenesis imperfecta and copper deficiency, can cause unexplained skeletal abnormalities.

The assessment should include a careful neurological examination, especially of the ocular fundi, to look for retinal hemorrhages, which may indicate a shaking injury or head trauma. It should go without saying that the physical examination must be performed calmly and gently so as not to distress the child.

Developmental Assessment

The time when a child is brought to medical attention with an injury that may be serious is not the best time to assess the child's development. However, it is important that a careful developmental assessment be done at some stage as part of the total assessment. Abused children may be fearful or sometimes delayed in their development, especially if both emotional abuse and neglect are present. Assessment of language development is important, as language delay is often seen in abused children.

Emotional Assessment

This may also have to be delayed until a more appropriate time, but should not be neglected. While it may not be particularly helpful in confirming the diagnosis of physical abuse, the emotional assessment is an important part of the total assessment, which becomes the basis for planning an appropriate treatment program for the child.

Assessment of Siblings

Other children in the family may have been physically abused, neglected, or emotionally abused. Even though the siblings may not have been injured, they may have experienced violence within the family and lived in a family that is stressful and dysfunctional. Information about the siblings should be collected and, if possible, they should also be assessed, particularly if there is any concern of danger to them. Features of abuse in other siblings would elevate the level of concern about parenting abilities in the family.

Protection for the Child

A decision has to be made as to whether it is safe for the child to return home or whether the child should be placed in a secure environment pending a full assessment of the family. If the child is to be kept from the parents, for example by being admitted to the hospital for treatment and observation, this should be discussed with the parents. Even though physical abuse can raise angry feelings in professionals, the parents have a right to be told calmly about the concerns and the reasons why the child will be temporarily separated from them. If the parents refuse to cooperate, it is usually possible to obtain a protective order from the social services department, although voluntary agreement often helps to avoid excessive antagonism between the parents and the professionals. This is important when the family becomes involved in treatment.

Assessment of the Family

Many professionals find this is best done in the company of another professional. It is a difficult area where emotions can run high. The presence of an additional professional may help the interview keep on track while useful feedback can be given in a debriefing session after the assessment. Assessment includes the parents' account of the circumstances surrounding the injury, their own background and childhood experiences, information about external pressures on them, and the availability and utilization of family and community supports. If there are two parents, they may be seen separately. Widely conflicting accounts of the injury by the parents should be a cause for concern. The coping skills of the parent or parents, along with their strengths and their relationship to the child, should be assessed in this interview.

Telling the Parents of Your Concern

If the physical features found in the child and the assessment of the parents suggest physical abuse, the parent or parents should be told òf this concern. This is always difficult but is far preferable to notifying the relevant social services authorities without informing the parents that this is being done. Telling the parents honestly of your concern can be the beginning of a trusting therapeutic relationship with the parents. It is helpful to remember that in general parents do not set out to hurt the child and that they do not hate the child. The injury usually occurs because the parents have a problem dealing with their own anger or aggressive tendencies or because of problems induced by external stresses. This perspective gives the parents and professional one common piece of ground with regard to the child: Both the parents and the professional want the child to grow up well and healthy without any further injury. Bringing this out into the open with the parents can be the beginning of the development of a therapeutic plan to achieve this aim.

All states in the United States, as well as several other countries, have mandatory notification legislation so that if abuse is thought to be likely, the relevant authority must be notified by the professional. The legislation usually includes indemnity against litigation concerning notification as long as the notification has been made in good faith. It is helpful to develop a professional working relationship with the relevant authorities so that all can work together in the child's best interests.

WORKING WITH OTHER PROFESSIONALS

Because physical abuse is a complex problem, several professional groups become involved in its management. Agendas or priorities can differ, such as investigation and prosecution, protection for the child, assessment of the family, provision of treatment for the child, and treatment for the family. These different views and agendas sometimes lead to conflict and lack of agreement. When this happens, the serious loser is usually the child, whose needs for protection and ongoing treatment may be overlooked. It takes time to develop the skill of working with other professionals and understanding their points of view. These are skills that should be cultivated by those working with abused children. A useful question to ask when there is a conflict of opinion is, "Which course of action would be in the best interests of the child, both for now and in the future?"

Case Conferences and Management Plans

A case conference is a useful way of bringing together the various professionals and agencies involved in the case. Although sometimes difficult to arrange and time consuming, case conferences have the advantage of allowing discussion of the case from a variety of viewpoints in order to make the most appropriate and realistic recommendations. Case conferences are usually held at a mutually convenient location, but can sometimes be arranged by telephone.

It is important that the recommendations made at case conferences be realistic and that it be clear which members of the group have responsibility for carrying out each specific recommendation. The plan of management decided at the case conference may include, for example, in the case of a child who returns home, such things as provision of home help; enrollment of the child in day care; help with some of the external stresses such as housing; help for the parents in developing a supportive network in the community; and assistance in improving their parenting skills.

The case conference should take place at the beginning of management rather than the end. The management plan created should be realistic and flexible, and should be reviewed and modified at regular intervals in order to respond to changes in circumstance.

It is more than 30 years since physical abuse was first comprehensively brought to the attention of professionals and then of the public. Much has been learned during this period about the types of injuries and the characteristics of the families involved. The challenge for the future is to learn more about how to use available resources most effectively and to develop the most appropriate forms of management and prevention strategies.

4

SEXUAL ABUSE

This chapter will concentrate on how to assess a case of possible child sexual abuse, including talking with the abused child and with the child's family, as well as discussing the principles involved in the physical assessment of the sexually abused child. It will then review some of the medical complications of child sexual abuse and some special and controversial areas, such as abuse caused by other children, abuse in nursery schools, abuse of children with special needs, ritual abuse, repressed memories, and giving evidence in court.

ASSESSING A CASE OF POSSIBLE SEXUAL ABUSE

Behavioral Pointers

The first indication that a child may have been sexually abused is sometimes a change in behavior or the development of a psychosomatic complaint as an indication of the child's distress. It is important to point out here that the presence of behavioral and psychosomatic pointers does not prove that there is child sexual abuse. Obviously, a whole variety of stresses in the child's life may be responsible for such symptoms or behaviors. The difference now is that, compared with the past when sexual abuse was seldom considered a possibility when psychosomatic disorders were assessed, child sexual abuse should be considered, along with other problems, as one of the possible causes of these symptoms. It is important to have an open mind when assessing child sexual abuse allegations, particularly when dealing with psychosomatic symptoms. This means not only a mind that is open to the possibility of sexual abuse, but also one that is not closed to other possibilities.

Nonspecific behavioral indicators may be recurrent abdominal pains or headaches. Recurrent abdominal pains are common between 5 and 10 years of age and occur in up to 10% of children. Organic causes (such as urinary tract infection or duodenal ulcer) are found in up to 10% of cases. Many of the remaining cases are thought to be due to underlying stress. Child sexual abuse should be considered as one of the stressors that may cause this condition. Recurrent headaches are also common, usually have no organic cause, and may represent a reaction to any one of a variety of stresses, one of which may be sexual abuse of the child.

Anorexia and other eating disorders may sometimes be a result of sexual abuse and should be considered when these conditions are being investigated. Similarly, enuresis (bed wetting), constipation, and encopresis (fecal withholding combined with soiling) can have a variety of causes, one of which may be child sexual abuse.

Sometimes, more specific behaviors are seen (Corwin, 1988). An adult may report sexualized behavior in a child. Such behaviors may include a preoccupation with the genitals; excessive or indiscreet masturbation or masturbation with objects; precocious, apparently seductive behavior; the involvement of other children in sexual behavior; and depicting sexual acts during play with dolls. The child may also show fearfulness and anxiety, and be troubled by nightmares. The problem is that such behavior can also be seen in children who have not been abused. There are no specific behavioral features that characterize victims of sexual abuse (Lamb, 1994). This means that the presence of these behaviors cannot be used to conclude that sexual abuse has taken place. Similarly, the absence of sexualized behavior does not confirm that sexual abuse did not take place. What sexualized behavior does provide is a sign that there may have been sexual abuse, suggesting the need for further investigation by personnel skilled in the assessment of sexual abuse in children and who are able to approach the question with an open mind.

Talking with the Child

In most cases of sexual abuse, only two people are certain as to whether or not the abuse occurred. One is the adult abuser. The other is the abused child. As most perpetrators are unwilling to admit the abuse, it is usually the child's account on which the clinician has to base a decision. This is particularly important, as often there is no physical evidence in child sexual abuse. As previously discussed (Chapter 2), the child may be reluctant to discuss the abuse because of fear of retribution or some other serious consequences from the abuser.

The interview with the child should be done in a relaxed manner that gives the child a feeling of trust and confidence in the interviewer. It is not good for the interview if the interviewer's anxiety is transmitted to the child. As well as a high order of clinical skills, another essential requirement is open-mindedness, meaning that the interviewer meets the child with no bias or preconceived view as to whether the child has been abused (Jones, 1990). The interviewer should have a good understanding of child development so as to be able to interpret different concepts and levels of understanding at different ages. Asking a 3-year-old about the days of the week on which an event occurred would be an example of lack of understanding of a child's developmental level.

Sometimes a child may make a spontaneous comment about sexual abuse to a professional who has not had particular training in talking about sexual abuse with young children. A mistake is to overreact to this comment, raising anxiety and alarm in the child. It is important to keep the line of communication open, encouraging the child to share more information without leading the child or making suggestions that could influence the child's account. It may then be appropriate to refer the child to a more experienced person.

Jones (1990) describes five phases in the interview conducted by professionals experienced in talking with children. In the first phase, the interviewer gains rapport with the child, discussing neutral aspects of the child's life, such as school and friends. The child may want to know if what she tells the interviewer will be told to others. The interviewer has to avoid the trap of promising confidentiality when this may not be possible.

In the second phase, there is some initial exploration about the possibility of sexual abuse. This may involve asking the child about her symptoms of anxiety or behavior, and may be enough to encourage the child's spontaneous discussion of an abusive event. If the child is reluctant to talk, the interview progresses to the phase of facilitation. Here the questions can be more specific, but must not be suggestive. A question such as, "Sometimes grown-ups play games with children that they don't like very much.... Has this happened to you?" is acceptable. Similarly, it may be reasonable to ask at some stage in the interview, "Has anyone ever touched inside your bottom?" This type of question is very different from the suggestive and less acceptable question, "Has Uncle John put his finger in your bottom?" Such a question may lead to an answer of "Yes," with Uncle John being falsely accused if the interviewer is demanding or if the young child is confused and intimidated. The child may then give an answer that she thinks the interviewer wants or may think that such an answer will mean that the questioning will stop. On the other hand, an answer of "No" to this question may wrongly exonerate Uncle John as young children are often quite literal in their interpretation. Uncle John may well have abused the child, but it may have been an object other than his finger that was inserted into the child's anus.

In this phase, anatomically correct dolls and other props may be used to help the child to convey an account. Such props can be helpful in determining the child's ability to name body parts and can be used in play to help children make verbal statements about events they have experienced. The interviewer should avoid naming the dolls as specific persons in the child's family. Sexualized play with dolls should be interpreted with caution. While sexualized play with dolls is more common among children who have been abused, some children who have not been abused may also play with dolls sexually. This means that sexualized play with dolls by itself should not be used to conclude that a child has been sexually abused, although the information can be helpful as the investigator tries to piece together the jigsaw about whether or not abuse has occurred. It is important to stress that there is no such thing as a test that can be done using anatomically detailed dolls to decide whether a child has been sexually abused (Everson & Boat, 1994).

Following facilitation, the fourth phase involves gathering specific details if sexual abuse has been described. These include such details as the type and pattern of abuse, the use of threats or coercion, the use of drugs or pornography, and the identity of the abuser. Finally, the interview should have a closing phase in which the interviewer reviews the main parts of the interview and acknowledges the feelings the child has struggled with and expressed.

A recent consensus statement on the investigation of child abuse (Lamb, 1994) recommends the following.

1. The child should be interviewed skillfully as soon as possible after the alleged incident has taken place.

2. Where possible, children should not be interviewed on multiple occasions as children's accounts, like those of adults, are at times suscep-

tible to "postevent contamination" where the report of an incident is distorted by the inclusion of details that were not part of the incident or of the original account.

3. To reduce the number of interviews, it is desirable to record primary investigative interviews, using audiotape or, preferably, videotape.

4. The most reliable and accurate information is obtained from children who are responding to open-ended questions designed to elicit free narrative accounts of events that they have experienced.

5. In young children (especially under 5 years of age), narrative information is likely to be limited and direct questions are needed to obtain further information.

6. When direct questions are asked, they should be nonsuggestive and use developmentally appropriate vocabulary and sentence construction. Whenever possible, direct questions should be followed by attempts to elicit free narrative.

7. Repeated, highly leading, or suggestive questions asked in an accusatory manner are ill advised because they are likely to promote distortion on the part of the child and may introduce details that become incorporated into and contaminate subsequent accounts.

Do Children Tell the Truth?

There has been considerable controversy about the credibility of child witnesses. In the adversarial legal system, questions are often raised about a child's reliability in testimony. When one examines the data on children's memory, a great deal is known and it is apparent that children, especially over 5 years of age, can be more reliable than was previously believed.

Most people who talk with children, including their

own, know that young children offer little information in free recall. This lack of spontaneous free recall by young children has given the impression that they remember little. This is an erroneous view. Most parents know that in response to a question to their own child, "What happened at school today," their child will often reply, "Nothing." However, if the parent asks some specific questions about games, classes, or teachers at the school, the child may provide a large amount of information.

There is also a view that children are more suggestible than adults. Most of the studies show that while children can be suggestible in some circumstances, children over 5 years are no more suggestible than adults and their memory for the central, more important aspects of an event in which they were involved is less likely to be influenced by suggestion than their memory for the more peripheral aspects of the event.

Studies that have involved children in an innocuous event and then attempted to create false reports of abuse through suggestive questioning show that children are more resistant to such questioning than was formerly believed. Caution has to be used when 3- or 4-year-old children are questioned. Although they can provide accurate memories of an event and although studies show that they rarely, if ever, give spontaneous reports of abuse, even under conditions of suggestive questioning, they do occasionally agree that abuse has occurred when it has not (Schwartz-Kenney, Wilson, & Goodman, 1990). It is clear from studies of suggestibility and its consequences for children's memory that children are more resistant to suggestions about abusive actions than would have been predicted from the earlier studies in which children's memory and suggestibility were tested for events they had observed but in which they had not personally been involved.

The increased knowledge about children's reliability as witnesses means that more children are now asked to testify in court. This raises the question as to whether testifying in court can itself be harmful to children. Children who have to testify may suffer stress from having to face the accused in the courtroom. One study (Weiss & Berg, 1982) found that sexually abused children who had given evidence in court had a delay in the resolution of negative symptoms caused by the abuse. On the other hand, Runyan and colleagues (1988) found that children who testified had a significant decrease in anxiety compared with those who did not, although in this study the children had testified in a juvenile rather than a criminal court. More recent evidence suggests that with appropriate supports, even in a criminal court, testifying need not be an adverse experience. Goodman and colleagues (1992) compared children who testified with those who did not at three points over time, the final one being at completion of the prosecution. No differences on behavioral measures were found between the two groups. A review of sexually abused children who testified at trial in Australia (Oates, Lynch, Stern, O'Toole, & Cooney, 1995) found that although 55% of parents expressed dissatisfaction with the legal system, thinking it was stressful to their children, a comparison of children who did not testify with those who did testify showed no significant differences between the two groups on indices of depression, self-esteem, or behavior. However, as most of these children had been involved in court-preparation programs and as most of the mothers were supportive of their children, these may have been ameliorating factors.

But, just because children who testify in court may appear to "get over" the experience, this is no reason not to make the experience less intimidating. The stress of giving evidence should be reduced by such reforms as preparation for court programs, the use of a screen between the child and the accused, and closed-circuit television that allows the child to give evidence from a room adjacent to the main courtroom.

Interviewing the Parents

The interview with the parent or parents of a sexually abused child provides information that not only may help to corroborate the child's disclosure about the abuse, but also clarifies the family dynamics and the question of how likely the family is to be able to protect the child from further abuse. Emotional tension on the part of the family may run high during the interview, not only when the abuse has been extrafamilial, causing anger in the parents, but also in intrafamilial abuse where there may be a desire to deny the abuse and to deny that there has been any emotional impact on the child.

The interview should be conducted calmly and professionally. The parents should be introduced to the interviewer or interviewers, be comfortably seated, and feel confident that privacy will be maintained as far as is legally possible. As taking notes during the interview may be distracting, it is helpful if the interview is videotaped. The parents should, of course, be aware of, and in agreement with, this form of recording.

The interviewer has four main tasks (Booth, 1990).

1. *Investigating the allegation.* This includes determining the parents' understanding of the allegation and gathering background information to clarify the story given by the child. Details of the relationship between the alleged offender and the child should be obtained, as well as details of access to the child. The parent will be able to give any information about behavioral changes seen in the child and it may be possible to relate the onset of these to the time when the abuse was thought to have commenced.

2. *Evaluation of family relationships and function.* Here, information about the family is obtained, such as relationships within the family, socioeconomic and cultural background, attitudes toward

sexuality and sexual behavior, changes in family structure, sleeping arrangements, and information about other adults who may move in and out of the family and about any custody disputes or access arrangements. Information about physical or mental health problems in the family should be explored, as well as whether the parents experienced sexual abuse in their own childhood. In particular it is helpful to know about the family's attitude to the child. Are they supportive of the child? Do they see the child as truthful, reliable, or easily led? Are the allegations believed by the family and what effect has this had on the family members?

3. *Evaluation of the parents' ability to protect the child.* The interviewer will need to know whether any action of the parents has placed the child at increased risk of abuse and whether the child will be able to be protected from further abuse, particularly if the abuse was intrafamilial. Families are sometimes angry with the child for revealing the abuse and deny that it is possible, even in the presence of strong evidence. They may victimize the child for making the allegations. These issues need to be explored at the interview to ensure that the child is protected not only from further sexual abuse but also from victimization.

4. *Counseling and support.* While it is hoped that the attitude of the interviewer and the conduct of the interview will have some therapeutic, as well as investigative, value, the interviewer should also determine the need for appropriate ongoing counseling, with specific recommendations made (at the end of the interview or later, if appropriate) about available services. These may include individual or group therapy for the child, as well as therapy and counseling for family members. This is especially important if the mother had been sexually abused in her own childhood, as she may

need help to see how her abuse may be influencing
the way she responds to her child's needs at this
time.

AVOIDING ERRORS

There are three common errors that have the potential for
causing problems in the assessment and treatment of child
sexual abuse cases.

Premature Intervention

It is well known that the disclosure of child sexual abuse
precipitates a crisis for the family. What is not as well
appreciated is that it can also precipitate a crisis for the
professional. Professionals often feel urged to act immediately when there is any suggestion of sexual abuse of a
child. Furniss (1990) draws a distinction between vague
"first-line suspicions" and well-founded "second-line suspicions," suggesting that a vague first-line suspicion should
be carefully documented and lead to further information
gathering and clarification, but should not be the basis for
triggering an immediate intervention with the child and
family. He believes that a first-line suspicion should
remain firmly within the professional network. Such a
suspicion may be an indication for a professional, such as
a teacher or doctor, to seek a consultation with another
experienced professional where the case can be discussed
in a problem-oriented way without necessarily naming
and identifying a child. Such a consultation helps the
professional to assess the reality of the initial suspicion
and how to establish the amount of further information
that may be necessary to reach a well-founded second-line
suspicion.

A pre-school child drew a man with what may have
been an erect penis. The teacher became concerned
about sexual abuse and called the child protective

services worker, who took the child into short-term placement and arranged for the family to be interviewed that evening. Much anger was generated, no additional evidence to support the suspicion was available, and the child developed a behavior disturbance as a result of the unplanned separation. Such an episode would have been avoided if the vague suspicion had been kept within the professional network, appropriate professional opinion sought, and a plan for gathering any further evidence, such as a relaxed, casual discussion of his drawings with the child, could have been developed.

Handing Cases over to Other Agencies

It is inevitable that some cases have to be passed on. This has the potential for disrupting the continuity of the intervention and the relationship of trust that should have been developed among the child, the family, and the professional. The potential problems can be avoided if the transfer is done with the family and both professionals present. This gives the family an opportunity to become aware that the outgoing professional has shared with the new professional the information the family provided. If this exchange of information is done in the family's presence, it helps the family to link with the new professional and gives them permission to continue the process of trust and communication that has been built. It is also important for the family to see that the professionals are in agreement and to avoid the easy trap of inferring that there is a "good professional" who has been replaced by a "bad professional" (Furniss, 1990) or vice versa.

Conflicts Between Professionals

Because of the variety of professional disciplines that become involved in child sexual abuse cases, there are often different perspectives. One professional's emphasis may be on protection of the child, another's may be on treatment of the family, whereas another may emphasize prosecution of the offender. Usually, when professional conflicts arise, it is the child who loses. Such conflicts are best resolved when various professionals learn to develop respect for each other and gain an understanding of differ-ent professional roles and responsibilities. Only after interprofessional conflicts are resolved will there be a genuine attempt to act in the child's best interests.

PHYSICAL INDICATORS
AND THE MEDICAL EXAMINATION

Specifics of the medical examination and anatomical find-ings will not be given in detail as they are well described in recent texts and journals (Bays & Chadwick, 1993; Emans & Heger, 1992; Hobbs, Hanks, & Wynne, 1993).

Knowledge about how best to examine sexually abused children is still evolving and many physicians are unaware of the normal variations in prepubertal anatomy. When Ladson, Johnson, and Doty (1987) surveyed pediatricians and family practitioners, they found that only 77% rou-tinely checked children's genitals more than half of the time. When asked to label anatomical parts on a picture of a 6-year-old girl's genitals, only 59% could correctly iden-tify the hymen. Eighty-nine percent identified the clitoris and 78% identified the urethral opening.

Even before the physical examination is done, there are some physical symptoms that may bring the child to medical care and may indicate sexual abuse. Vaginal bleeding is an important indicator of possible abuse that must always be investigated. Such bleeding occasionally is caused by an accident, although there should be a history of a painful fall, usually a straddle injury. Other causes include early onset of puberty and some medical disorders. Similarly, sexual abuse should always be considered when rectal bleeding is present. Other causes of rectal bleeding include an anal fissure, which itself may be caused by abuse; infective diarrhea; rectal polyps; or inflammatory bowel disorder. Although sexual abuse must be considered an important and common cause of vaginal or rectal bleeding, it should be emphasized that most cases of child sexual abuse do not cause bleeding. Vulvovaginitis and a vaginal discharge can have a variety of causes, such as poor hygiene and dermatological disorders; although sexual abuse should always be considered and discharges should be cultured to look for an infective cause, including sexually transmitted diseases.

Sexually transmitted disease is an extremely strong indicator of child sexual abuse, as it is extremely rare for it to be transmitted by nonsexual means. Pregnancy is, of course, an obvious indicator of abuse. When a general physical examination reveals bruises, bites, and scratches on the lower abdomen and inner aspects of the thighs, the possibility of sexual abuse should be considered.

Some of the general principles in the medical diagnosis of child sexual abuse have been described by Bays and Chadwick (1993).

1. A normal physical examination is common in child sexual abuse because much sexual abuse does not involve penetration. Even when it does, injuries involving the vaginal and rectal areas heal quickly.

2. In the absence of congenital anomalies, all girls are born with a hymen. Total or partial absence of the hymen implies its disruption by abuse or accident, abuse being the far more common cause.

3. Normal hymens have various configurations, so physicians should be aware of the normal variations.

4. The appearance of the hymen and the size of the hymenal opening change with different positions and different examination techniques.

5. Accidents, masturbation, and the use of tampons are very unlikely to cause injury to the hymen or to the internal genital structures.

6. The size of the normal hymenal opening increases

with age. Although hymen openings have been shown to be larger in abused compared with nonabused girls, it is difficult to use this as a "test" for sexual abuse. A recent consensus statement on assessment of child sexual abuse (Lamb, 1994) asserted: "The size of the hymenal orifice is no longer viewed as a reliable indicator of abuse" (p. 1026). This also means that a relatively small hymenal opening does not exclude abuse since the opening of an injured hymen may become smaller following healing. Basing a diagnosis of sexual abuse using the size of the hymenal orifice as the sole indicator is fraught with danger. The diagnosis of sexual abuse is made "not on a genital measurement, but on descriptive statements made by a child" (Paradise, 1989, p. 176).

7. Transmission of sexually transmitted disease outside the perinatal period by nonsexual means is a rare occurrence.

THE PHYSICAL EXAMINATION OF THE SEXUALLY ABUSED CHILD

The physical examination of a sexually abused child should be done with the child's permission in an atmosphere of calm and reassurance. It should be performed by a person with skills and training in this area and as soon as possible after the alleged incident. The examination should be preceded by an explanation to the child, which should emphasize that the assessment will be made based on "looking" rather than on "touching." It is preferable to start with a full general physical examination, checking general health and looking for evidence of abuse in other areas. After this has been done, genital inspection is usually adequate. With females, this part of the examination should include more than one position to increase the certainty about the presence or absence of physical signs.

There are two commonly used positions: In the first, the child lies on her back. Gentle separation and traction of the labia give a good view of the tissues surrounding the vagina. In the other position, the child lies on her front in the knee-to-chest position so that the vaginal opening can be inspected from behind. This position gives a good view of the hymen. Penetration of the vagina usually tears the hymen and occasionally other tissues if penetration has been forceful. The tears are usually found between the 3:00 o'clock and 9:00 o'clock position on the posterior rim of the hymen. These tears will heal in 5 to 10 days with the sharp edges of the separated hymen rounding off over the next few months.

Anal injuries are less common since relatively gentle penetration of the anus, especially if lubrication is used, causes little damage.

Often, a magnifying device with the ability to photograph, such as a colposcope, can be used to improve visualization and to record the findings. Photographs can be particularly useful in demonstrating changes, such as healing over time.

Usually, forensic specimens for semen and for evidence of sexually transmitted disease should be obtained and follow-up is necessary to see whether sexually transmitted disease has been contracted. It is essential to meticulously record the findings of the assessment, including verbatim recordings of significant statements made by the child during examination.

Although most cases of child sexual abuse have no physical findings so that the history must be relied upon to reach a decision about the abuse, there are some medical findings that are diagnostic for sexual abuse, even in the absence of a history of abuse. These have been described by Bays and Chadwick (1993).

1. The presence of semen, sperm, or acid phosphatase in the genital tract
2. Pregnancy

3. Fresh genital or anal injuries (such as cuts, abrasions, bruises, petechiae, and bite marks) in the absence of an adequate accidental explanation

4. A positive test for syphilis or gonorrhea, assuming it was not acquired around the time of birth

5. HIV infection if not acquired by the intravenous route or around the time of birth

6. A markedly enlarged hymenal opening for age, with associated findings of hymen disruption, including absence of the hymen, hymenal remnants, and healed transections or scars in the absence of an adequate accidental or surgical explanation

MEDICAL COMPLICATIONS

The major medical complications of child sexual abuse are acute injury, pregnancy, and sexually transmitted disease.

Acute Injury

In most cases of child sexual abuse, even when there is penetration, the injury, while diagnostically significant, is usually not medically significant. However, violent sexual assault can result in acute injury, including serious genital, anal, and other physical injury. Usually, for the physical examination, genital inspection is adequate, although if there is evidence of significant internal injury, the child should be examined under general anesthesia and the opportunity taken to repair any significant injury, such as rectovaginal tears or rupture of the vaginal vault.

Pregnancy

When pregnancy is a possibility, the use of pregnancy prophylaxis should be considered. Pregnancy is a possibility in pubertal females, where there has been penetration during midcycle and where there is no regular contraception in use. There are various regimes available, usually based on a high-estrogen, combined pill. As nausea can be an unpleasant side effect of the treatment, it is best given with an antiemetic (Kovacs, et al. 1984).

Sexually Transmitted Diseases

It is part of the physician's responsibility to detect and treat any sexually transmitted disease in a sexually abused child. Infections include gonorrhea, chlamydia, herpes simplex, bacterial vaginosis (a syndrome where there is an overgrowth of multiple organisms), human papilloma virus (producing genital warts), trichomonas vaginalis, syphilis, and HIV infection. The symptoms vary with the condition, from a discharge in symptomatic cases of gonorrhea (although up to 45% of children infected with gonorrhea can have no symptoms) to the long, silent period of several years with HIV infection. Sexually transmitted disease should be considered in all cases of child sexual abuse and appropriate investigations and treatment carried out. A full description of sexually transmitted diseases following sexual abuse in children and an approach to their management is provided by Stewart (1992).

SPECIAL SITUATIONS

Abuse by Other Children

In some cases of sexual abuse, the offender may be a child. When one is evaluating sexual interactions between children, many of which may be normal exploratory behavior, the behavior would be considered abusive if there are elements of lack of consent, coercion, and inequality (such as in terms of age or power) between the children. Intervention is required because it has been shown that many sexual abusers develop their patterns of deviant behavior before their late teenage years (Abel, Rouleau, & Cunningham-Rathner, 1986).

In the Extrafamilial Molestation Project at the Kempe National Center for the Prevention and Treatment of Child Abuse and Neglect, 33% of the children who had been sexually abused outside the family had been molested by youths who were on average 14 years of age (Ryan, Metzner, & Krugman, 1990). The juvenile sex offender does not have an identifiable profile. Ryan et al. (1990) summarized what is known about them. Over 70% live at home with their parents at the time of offending. Less than 10% are in placement, such as foster care. Seventy percent have an average or better-than-average school performance, although 72% also show behavior problems or learning difficulties on their school reports. Between 39% and 70% were victims of sexual abuse as young children, with 40% reporting physical abuse as well. Many have a poor self-image, feel a lack of control in their lives, and expect problems to occur. Many deny or minimize the abuse. Treatment of these juveniles is important if the chance of their repeating the abuse is to be reduced. Preliminary information (Ryan et al., 1990) suggests that they require long-term, offence-specific intervention utilizing a mixture of cognitive, behavioral, educational, and psychodynamic methods.

Abuse in Nursery Schools

Child abuse in nursery schools and day-care centers has only been relatively recently recognized. Finkelhor and Williams (1988a) estimated that, in 1985, 1300 children were sexually abused in 267 day-care centers and family day-care groups in the United States. Perpetrators may hold any position: the owner of the facility, a staff member such as a teacher, a nonprofessional child-care staff member, a staff member's relative, or a staff member not involved in child care. In contrast to some of the widely publicized preschool abuse cases, in the majority of instances, the abuse involves only a single perpetrator.

In Finkelhor and Williams' study, it was found that 40% of the abusers in day-care centers were female, a much higher percentage than is usually found in sexual abuse cases and presumably accounted for by the fact that only 5% of day-care staff are male. In two thirds of cases, the abuse occurred at times when the children were being taken to the toilet, an ideal time for an abuser to be alone with a child and where some undressing of the child is normally expected. In 93% of cases, there was some form of penetration. In 13% of cases, there were allegations of ritual abuse.

These cases of day-care abuse came to attention in a variety of ways. In 37%, disclosure was a result of the child's spontaneously telling what had happened. In most other cases, parents became suspicious because of fear, sexual behavior, or physical symptoms. The most common symptoms among abused children may be fears and sleep disturbances, followed by aggressive behavior and inappropriate sexual behavior. As a result of their study, Finkelhor and Williams (1988b) made a series of recommendations aimed to reduce both the incidence of children being abused in day-care situations and the incidence of false allegations, thus providing some protection for staff.

1. Preventive education to preschool children with emphasis on having no secrets in day-care; the importance of telling their parents about unusual behaviors they may be asked to participate in, and the fact that they are safe from any threats from day-care staff once they are at home.

2. Day-care centers should develop policies and architectural designs that prevent abuse in the bathroom. This may involve removing partitions that create private areas and establishing policies regarding toilet supervision procedures.

3. Licensing authorities should screen household members and extended family who have access to the children, as well as staff actually employed in the center. This screening should look at a broad range of background information, such as emotional disorders, criminal behavior, a punitive attitude toward children, and substance abuse. This would be in place of merely looking for a history of pedophilia, as this is uncommon in most day-care sex abusers.

4. As parents are usually the first to become aware of the abuse, they should be taught to be more aware of warning signs, such as unusual fears, genital irritation, or unusual sexual knowledge.

5. Education for day-care staff about the signs and symptoms of sexual abuse in children should be provided.

6. Day-care facilities should develop an approved plan for responding to allegations of sexual abuse.

7. Child protective service teams in the community should develop plans for the most appropriate way to investigate allegations of sexual abuse in day-care centers, with emphasis on knowledge of child development and children's testimony.

One problem is that many of the nonspecific symptoms of sexual abuse, such as nightmares, fears, and separation anxiety may occur in the normal course of a child's development and often have their origin in things other than sexual abuse. The clinician should keep an open mind when the possibility of sexual abuse is raised in day care and will have to work with the parent and child to differentiate benign symptoms from ones that may be a reaction to abuse. A single symptom is rarely diagnostic of abuse, but it can be the clue to see if there is a pattern of symptoms that may suggest that abuse has taken place (Kelly, Brant, & Waterman, 1993).

Although sexual abuse occurs in many day-care situations, parents need to be aware that the risk is relatively low, despite media attention. For example, in the year of the Finkelhor survey, whereas an estimated 1300 children were sexually abused in day-care centers, approximately 100,000 were sexually abused by family members.

Abuse of Children with Special Needs

It is difficult enough to make a diagnosis of sexual abuse in a normal child. The difficulties when the child is handicapped, especially with poor communication skills, are even greater. It is now being recognized that these children are at greater risk than are children in the normal population. Ammerman et al. (1989) found that of 150 children with multiple handicaps admitted to a residential hospital, 30% had been abused. Of those who were sexually abused, multiple perpetrators had been involved in 40% of cases. The sexual abuse had occurred before 2 years of age in 50% of cases and had involved penetration in two thirds.

Children with special needs are vulnerable because abusers know that their communication problems make it unlikely that the abuse will be detected. These children are dependent on others for dressing, washing, and toileting, and often have multiple people involved in their care over the years, increasing the chance of one of these people being an abuser. In addition, many of the children have a need for affection that is exploited by the abuser. They are inexperienced and do not know about normal behavior, while some of their behavior disturbances, at times a result of the abuse, are wrongly attributed to their underlying disorder (Schor, 1987).

These children should be assessed by a person skilled in communicating with children who have the particular disorder. The use of props, drawings, and play may be helpful, although there is a need to be aware of the dangers of overinterpretation. One method coming into use recently to help these children express themselves is facilitated communication, which involves having the child select symbols or words (such as from a picture board, word list, or electronic communication aid) by touching or pointing. Because of the extent of the handicap, the facilitator is often required to support the child's arm so that the child can move the arm or finger to the selected response. Problems have arisen because, using facilitated communication, children at times have related experiences of sexual abuse using adult concepts, words, and sentence structures that would not have been expected to be in their vocabulary. This raises the question of whether the facilitator is consciously or unconsciously influencing the child's response.

Heckler (1994), exploring the communicative abilities of autistic children where facilitated communication has produced sexual abuse allegations, has not found any evidence that the allegations have emerged from the autistic children independently. They appear to have derived from the facilitator. This is in keeping with most of the research evidence so far (Jones, 1994). Although facilitated communication may be a useful tool for enabling severely handicapped children to communicate, it still needs to be evaluated more carefully before it can be relied on for the diagnosis of sexual abuse. The whole area of facilitated communication was thoughtfully reviewed in the journal *Child Abuse and Neglect* (vol. 18, no. 6, 1994).

Allegations or suspicions of child sexual abuse in children with special needs, as well as being investigated by history, should also be investigated by physical examination when indicated. This is done in the usual way, although extra care may be needed to comfort and reassure the child. As many of these children have had multiple abusive experiences, including a high incidence of penetration, the likelihood of positive findings should be higher than in other situations, although there have been no good comparative studies.

The prevention of abuse in these children begins with

the acceptance, unpalatable as it may seem, that this group of children is at particular risk. This involves education of these children, their parents, and professionals about protection and prevention, along with recommendations similar to those that have been made to reduce the incidence of abuse in day-care centers.

RITUAL ABUSE

The terms "ritualistic abuse" and "satanic abuse" lead to high levels of anxiety in parents, professionals, and the community. They also lead to enthusiastic, often sensational, reporting in the media. Ritual abuse is an extreme end of the spectrum of child abuse and most likely is only a small part of the total problem. However, its sensational aspects may give it undue prominence. Ritual abuse is defined by Finkelhor and Williams (1988c, p. 59) as "abuse that occurs in the context linked with some symbols or group activities that may have a religious, magical or supernatural connotation and where the invocation of these symbols or activities are repeated over time and used to frighten and intimidate the children." They suggest that there are three subtypes:

1. True cult-based, where the sexual abuse is just one component of the child's total immersion in cult rituals and beliefs
2. Pseudoritualistic, where the sexual abuse is the primary activity and cult rituals are secondary to this
3. Psychopathological ritualism, where an adult, alone or with others, abuses the child in a ritualistic fashion that is a result of obsessive or delusional systems

Jones (1991) believes that ritualistic abuse can have serious effects. The embedding of the sexual abuse within a powerful, often deviant, belief system may create long-lasting distortion of the victim's beliefs and fundamental personality structure so that recovery is difficult. The combination of the abuse with sadistic, premeditated activity seems to result in serious psychological effects and the extreme degradation of the victim may have serious consequences for the development of self-esteem.

When an allegation of some form of ritual abuse is made, especially if it involves significant numbers of children, the professionals are quickly divided into two groups, one that believes the allegation, and the other that does not (Jones, 1991). Jones points out that outside expert help is often brought in too late and that in the meantime the parents have formed their own network, with the potential problem of contamination of the children's evidence. There is intense media interest, the professionals start to criticize each other, and "finally the situation ends with wide disbelief, suggestions of mass hysteria and bruised professionals, pediatricians and children" (Jones, 1991).

Some of the stories children relate may be difficult to believe. They may include infant sacrifice, the drinking of blood and urine, the use of drugs, dressing up in robes, chanting, and a variety of invasive and degrading sexual activities. The sources of evidence for these claims may be the children themselves, adults who claim ritual abuse in their childhood, witnesses to the abuse, admissions by perpetrators, and evidence from police investigation, although the majority of police investigations have provided little evidence. Jones (1991) describes three possible explanations:

1. The events occurred exactly as described. A problem with this possibility is the absence of verification by police investigation.
2. The event did not happen at all. This may be possible in some cases, although unlikely for all of the reports, as the allegations are so detailed and often consistent among the children.

3. Some of the events actually occurred and others are fictitious. This is also a likely possibility. The use of drugs may confuse the child, the abuser may deliberately use tactics to make the child's account seem fanciful, and the psychological abuse and degradation may be so overwhelming that they distort the child's memory.

The confusion in this area points out the need for extremely careful, nonleading interviewing in such cases, along with early expert advice and measures to avoid contamination.

REPRESSED MEMORIES

Many adults are now said to be recalling abusive experiences in their own childhood that had previously been repressed. There is skepticism about all of these memories being accurate, with the concern that at times therapists may be suggesting that past, repressed sexual abuse could be responsible for their clients' current problems. It is possible for memory of childhood sexual abuse to be completely repressed. This is known from cases where the information is corroborated by the abuser or by another family member (Matthews, 1990). However, in most cases there is no corroboration, many years have passed, and, like most child sexual abuse cases, it is the word of the victim against the word of the alleged offender. Some cases of repressed memory can be corroborated, other cases can be shown to be false. In the great majority of cases, it is difficult to be sure. Given the present state of knowledge, we do not know whether to believe a majority or a minority of the repressed memories of child sexual abuse. It is a particularly difficult area, one that calls for therapists to be very careful about suggesting the possibility of past sexual abuse and for investigators to carefully consider the rights of all parties involved.

TESTIFYING IN COURT

Many of those who see sexually abused children are asked
to testify in court. In some cases, the facts are clear and
definite statements can be made about the child's developmental level, behavior, and any physical findings. This
information assists the court in reaching an appropriate
decision. At other times, the facts of the case are less clear
and the expert's interpretation of them is more difficult
(Oates, 1993).

It is important for the professional called to give evidence in court to be objective. The job of the witness is to
help the court and the jury by being accurate and balanced.
For example, in quoting literature about sexual abuse, the
witness should not fall into the trap of quoting only those
aspects of a particular paper that would advance the cause
of the party calling the witness, ignoring other aspects that
may be less favorable to the case. If a different point of view
exists, that may need to be given too. As decisions made as
a result of a professional's testimony may seriously affect
people's lives, it is important to stick to the facts and not to
exaggerate. A good rule to work by is that the statements
made in court should reflect the same quality and level of
scholarship that would be deemed appropriate for a scientific seminar or for publication in a reputable journal.

Witnesses should also stick to their area of expertise. To
be flattered into giving an opinion in an area where a
witness has little experience is a trap wherein one runs the
risk of having counsel point out to the court that the
opinion is without foundation. This is an effective way of
destroying a witness's credibility even in areas in which
the witness has real expertise.

Professionals who give evidence are sometimes manipu-
lated into a partisan position. It is important to remember
that the expert's job is not to win or lose the case; rather, it
is to make available knowledge and expertise that can
assist the court in interpreting facts in complex issues. A

final tip is not to appear as an expert witness too often. Although appearing as an expert witness is an important part of one's professional responsibility, it should be a minor part of one's professional activities. It is difficult to claim in court that one is a clinician or therapist active in the area or a scholar up to date with the latest research if most of one's time is spent going from court to court as an expert witness.

5

EMOTIONAL ABUSE AND NEGLECT

Although neglect and emotional abuse of children are common, these are conditions that usually cause no physical signs and are subtler in their manifestations than physical abuse or sexual abuse. For these reasons, such abuse tends to come to the attention of professionals less often and, in the case of emotional abuse, recognition of its extent and seriousness has been slow. Emotional abuse can be regarded as an underlying characteristic of all forms of child abuse. Children who are physically injured by their parents or caretakers and children who are sexually misused for the emotional gratification of an adult are also emotionally abused as a result of these acts. The adult who sexually misuses a child is giving that child a message that her value to the adult is not as a person, but as something the adult can use for his own satisfaction.

In this chapter, emotional abuse will be reviewed, followed by a discussion of neglect, with particular emphasis on one aspect of neglectful behavior causing growth failure (nonorganic failure to thrive) in infants.

THE REQUIREMENTS FOR GOOD MENTAL HEALTH

The foundations for good mental health are usually laid down in infancy. Bowlby (1951) believed that for good mental health and development the infant and young child should experience a warm, intimate, and continuous relationship with the mother or other appropriate caretaker. Rutter (1972) listed the following characteristics as being necessary for adequate mothering or parenting, the absence of which could lead to emotional deprivation or neglect. The underlying requirement is that there should be a loving relationship that:

1. leads to attachment.
2. is unbroken.
3. provides adequate stimulation for the child.
4. has mothering provided by one person.
5. occurs in the child's own family.

Children also have to have their other needs met, such as the provision of adequate nutrition, having opportunities for conversation and play with children and adults, being protected from danger, and having discipline based mainly on teaching and role models.

Not all children have all of these needs adequately met, and there is a variation in how children respond to such deficiencies. Some seem to fare worse than others. Children have a mixture of strength and vulnerability. They are able to influence their parents' behavior and in turn they develop according to the way their parents behave toward them. This has been described using an example of a crying infant (Solnit, 1984). The normal behavior of an infant may be seen by one set of parents as being healthy. Another set of parents may see this normal behavior as being sick, whereas yet another pair may see this behavior as violent. The parents who are aware of normal infant behavior will see the crying and fussiness, which all infants experience, as normal and will soothe the child. The second set of parents may think that the crying and fussiness are due to an illness and will be reassured only when the child has been checked and declared well. The third set of parents, whose own needs for dependency are great and who fear the demands of their infant, will see the crying baby as demanding. They may become locked into a vicious cycle where the infant's behavior evokes tense responses, leading to increased crying and perhaps even to a situation that puts the infant at risk for abuse and neglect. There is still a great deal to learn about why some children seem resilient and some more vulnerable when exposed to similar circumstances in their childhoods.

EMOTIONAL ABUSE

Emotional abuse is a hidden form of child abuse. It differs from neglect in that with emotional abuse there is some deliberate action on the part of the parent against the child. When emotional abuse manifests as a behavior disorder, the underlying cause is often not recognized. Yet this form of abuse may be even more damaging than physical abuse and neglect.

Types of Emotional Abuse

Garbarino, Guttman, & Seeley (1986) have defined psychological maltreatment or emotional abuse as a concerted attack by an adult on a child's development of self and social competence. They have provided a helpful classification of emotional abuse that describes different types of adult behavior. This classification helps further an understanding of the responses children have to different types of emotional abuse. Five types of emotional abuse are described.

1. *Rejecting.* This involves behaviors that communicate or constitute abandonment of the child, such as the adult's refusing to touch or show affection to the child. In this way, the adult is

refusing to acknowledge the child's worth and needs.

2. *Terrorizing.* Here, the child is threatened with extreme and sometimes sinister punishment. This behavior intentionally stimulates intense fear in the child. It creates a climate of unpredictable threat where expectations that are unable to be met are set and where the child is punished for not being able to meet them. As a result, the child comes to believe that the world is unpredictable and hostile.

3. *Ignoring.* The adult is psychologically unavailable to the child. This is often so because the adult is so preoccupied with personal needs that there is no ability to respond to the child's behavior. Depriving the child of stimulation in this way interferes with the child's intellectual and emotional growth.

4. *Isolating.* The adult prevents the child from taking advantage of normal opportunities for social reaction. The child has limited opportunities to form friendships and comes to feel alone in the world.

5. *Corrupting.* Here, the adult behaviors give the child false social values reinforcing antisocial or deviant patterns, especially aggression, drug abuse, and deviant sexuality.

To better understand these five forms of emotional abuse, Garbarino et al. (1986) believe they should be looked at in each of the four major stages of development: the first 2 years, years 2 to 5, the early school years, and adolescence.

They discuss how these types of emotional maltreatment can take different forms, depending on the age of the child. For example, rejection in infancy may mean refusal to respond to the child's smiles and vocalizations. Rejection in adolescence may mean subjecting the adolescent to humiliating and excessive criticism. Similarly, isolation in early childhood may involve punishing the child for making social overtures to children and adults, whereas for the school-age child it may mean preventing the child from playing with other children or inviting them home.

These behaviors have important consequences for the emotional development of children. During the first year of life, when children are developing the concept of trust, adult behaviors, such as rejecting or ignoring, are likely to develop in the child the view that people are unreliable and cannot be trusted. In the 2-to-5-year age group, when children start to develop autonomy and later learn the value of initiating their own activities, adult behaviors, such as terrorizing and ignoring, are likely to stifle initiative and interfere with the development of self-esteem. The school-age and adolescent child learns to mix socially, to compete, and to develop strong peer-group relationships. Adult behaviors, such as isolating, will interfere with this developmental process, while corrupting may ensure that whatever relationships are formed are likely to be antisocial and deviant.

Clearly, then, the way children respond to emotional abuse will depend on the type of abuse and the age of the child. Infants who are emotionally maltreated usually respond by being apathetic or irritable and difficult to calm. This response is likely to increase the emotionally abusive behavior of the parents. Because parents do not respond appropriately, these infants do not learn to act in the way Brazelton (1982) has described as "taking turns," where the parent's and the infant's movements and vocalizations are in harmony with each other. Older children come to see the world as a place hostile to them. They become distrustful and so are difficult to help. They tend to have low self-esteem and a negative view of the world, sometimes mixed with anxiety and antisocial behavior. These effects can be lifelong and so interfere with the child's ability to form satisfactory relationships through-out childhood and in adult life.

Characteristics of the Parents

A common feature in parents or adults who emotionally abuse their children is that they often do not know enough about child development to cope with the normal demands resulting from their child's behavior at different developmental stages. They may also tend to isolate themselves from the community. This can be a two-way process, as the behavior of these parents may lead to the family being ignored by neighbors and the community.

Emotional maltreatment seems to occur more often in poorer communities where there is high unemployment, poverty, and a sense of powerlessness and frustration among the parents (Brown, 1984). However, it is also probably easier to detect in poorer communities. Emotional abuse also is found in middle-and upper-class families where there are stress, tension, and aggression coupled with inadequate parenting skills and unrealistic expectations of the children. Middle-and upper-class families may be better able to hide the emotional abuse of their children, and the professionals treating these children may be more reluctant to consider this diagnosis.

Parental behaviors seen in emotionally abusive families include being unable to meet their children's psychological needs, responding inappropriately to their children by giving them too many responsibilities and punishing them when they fail, inappropriately infantilizing their children so that they are prevented from reaching their potential, lacking respect for their children's thoughts and feelings, and being inconsistent in parenting so that the children receive conflicting and contradictory messages and see their parents as unreliable (Herrenkohl, Herrenkohl, & Egolf, 1981; Egeland, Stroufe, & Erickson, 1983; Patterson & Thompson, 1980).

In a study to compare emotionally abusive parents and

children with other families, a group of emotionally abusing parents were compared with a closely matched control
group of problem parents in a day nursery (Brazelton,
1982). The emotionally abusing parents showed poorer
coping skills, poorer child management techniques, and
more difficulty in forming relationships. They also reported more deviant behavior in their children than did the
control parents.

The Professional's Response to Emotional Abuse

As with other forms of abuse, an important initial aspect of
intervention is a careful assessment of the family. This will
determine what type of intervention is needed and whether
this can be done with family cooperation or whether legal
backing is necessary to do. Because some of the problems
in emotionally abusing families are related to stress, it may
be important to focus at first on some of the family's
concrete problems, such as material resources, as this
approach is likely to be more acceptable to the family.
Treatment aimed solely at family dynamics and that ignores some of the family's practical needs is less likely to
be successful. It is important that any interventions have
realistic goals aimed to meet the needs of the parents and
the children.

Simply making suggestions to improve family functioning may not be enough. Practical help may also be needed.
Practical home-based services for neglectful families have
been shown to support and improve the functioning of
families that would otherwise have had their children
removed from home. They are more cost-effective than
placing the child in care (Van Meter, 1986).

Other interventions may include marital counseling,
family therapy, neighborhood support systems, home visits, and helping the parents to more accurately understand
their children's development and behavior so that they can
come to tolerate the child's curiosity, exploration, and
failures as the young child develops and tries to master the

environment. Helping the parents to understand, rather than to misinterpret, these normal behaviors, and providing them with resources to cope with them can be an effective method of intervention in families who have some degree of motivation.

Intervention with the child may involve play therapy, day care, the use of a therapeutic preschool where the child can learn from alternative role models, and training in social skills and interventions to help the child to develop and improve self-esteem. Ideally, parent and child treatments should proceed simultaneously so that parental confidence and self-esteem are improved at the same time these gains are made in the child.

In addition to prevention at the individual level, it has been suggested that prevention should be considered at the level of the social system in society to encompass the fundamental cultural beliefs we hold about children (Lally, 1984). At the level of government assistance, families usually come to the attention of governments only when problems arise. Policy is generally set to react to problems rather than to ensure that systems are available to help families and children when economic factors, such as inflation, recession, and underemployment, affect them. At a community level, while the family is the basic unit, there is a place for larger systems, such as neighborhood and community resources, to become involved in helping families to cope more effectively.

NEGLECT

Neglect results from inadequate or negligent parenting. Some aspects of neglect may seem obvious. A child may be not well cared for, may be inadequately clothed, not receive quality food, and be delayed in developmental milestones, especially language skills. A potential error is overzealousness in the detection of neglect, leading to the confusion of neglect with poverty or ignorance. In a family that is poor, with insufficient shelter, no regular income, and generally overwhelmed by circumstances, there may be children who are poorly clothed and underfed and perhaps not very clean. To label this family as neglectful when they are in circumstances over which they have little control is unfair. These families need help; only if they refuse reasonable services to help their children should neglect be considered. Schmitt (1981) has divided neglect into five categories: medical neglect, safety neglect, educational neglect, physical neglect, and emotional neglect.

Medical Neglect

Medical practitioners are most likely to be aware of medical neglect. This can include refusing blood transfusions for religious reasons, refusing childhood immunizations because of erroneous beliefs that they are dangerous, and refusing to sign consent forms for other necessary and perhaps lifesaving interventions. Court intervention is often necessary to solve these problems. However, undue conflict with the parents should be avoided and, where possible, they should be included in careful discussion, rather than shut out by argument, and they should be involved in the decision-making process even when this involves legal intervention.

Medical neglect can also include refusing to give regular medication for chronic conditions, such as diabetes mellitus (sometimes done on religious grounds), embarking on bizarre diets that may lead to vitamin deficiency and anemia, and refusing proved medical treatment in favor of unproved, unorthodox treatments for chronic or potentially fatal diseases. This becomes particularly complex when parents want to try unorthodox treatments in cases of malignant disease. When the standard treatment offers a reasonable chance of cure, and when the parents wish to abandon this in favor of an unproved treatment, legal intervention may be needed to ensure that the child is treated optimally. Potential problems can often be overcome if the medical practitioner makes sure that the parents have plenty of opportunities to ask questions so as to understand the treatment, that they have the material resources to be able to comply with the treatment, and that other assistance, such as interpreters and relatives or trusted friends, is provided to help the parents understand the treatment. This is especially important if they have misapprehensions based on past experience, cultural beliefs, or language barriers

Safety Neglect

This type of neglect occurs when the child suffers as a result of a marked lack of supervision. It is sometimes difficult to distinguish between accidents that could not likely have been prevented and accidents occurring as a result of the parent or caretakers not taking adequate measures to protect the child.

> The mother of a 3-year-old youngster left her child at home alone for two hours while she went out for a drink with her friends. An electric heater was turned on in the room. The infant put a stool next to the electric heater and then dropped a blanket between the stool and the heater to make a playhouse. The blanket caught fire and the child suffered extensive, disfiguring burns.

Close supervision and the careful monitoring of the child's environment to remove hazards and avoid dangerous situations are essential in the early years of life.

Educational Neglect

With educational neglect, the child is kept away from school, sometimes to work at home or to do baby sitting. The parent may exaggerate a minor illness in order to keep the child at home for long periods. Another example would be the parent who colludes with a child who has school phobia, rather than seeking medical treatment.

Physical Neglect

Physical neglect means that the child's basic needs for food, shelter, and clothing are not met. This is neglect only if the family has the material resources to provide these essentials for the child but neglects to do so.

Emotional Neglect

Emotional neglect is similar to emotional abuse discussed earlier in this chapter. It leads to withdrawal, delay in language and motor development, and sometimes inappropriate displays of affection toward strangers. Infants who are emotionally neglected are more likely than other infants (but not exclusively so) to use persistent, self-stimulating behavior, such as rocking or head banging. They also appear to be insecure in their play and behavior. In contrast to abused infants, whose play is likely to have a high activity level, but which is not of high quality and is sometimes destructive, neglected infants are more likely to have low levels of play behavior, to be passive, and sometimes to show little interest in toys. Language delay is also common in neglected children. Some emotionally neglected children have features of nonorganic failure to thrive.

NONORGANIC FAILURE TO THRIVE

Deprivation of Calories or of Affection?

Initially, there was conflicting evidence about whether the growth failure of certain infants was due to deprivation of affection and stimulation or was simply a result of deprivation of calories. Early studies of infants separated from their mothers (Spitz, 1945) and of older children from orphanages in postwar Germany (Widdowson, 1951) claimed that the depriving and harsh environments, rather than lack of food, were responsible for the growth failure. However, no analysis of actual food intake was reported in these studies.

In one study, which would be unlikely to gain ethical approval in the 1990s, 13 infants with nonorganic failure to thrive were kept for two weeks in a windowless room where they received minimal handling but an adequate diet. Despite the emotional and sensory deprivation, all but three infants had an accelerated weight gain. Six of these infants then received a high level of mothering and sensory stimulation, but without any improvement in their diet. There was no change in their rate of weight gain. The conclusion from this study was that if children are given enough food, they will grow, and that the problem of growth failure in maternal deprivation is due to inadequate caloric intake (Whitten, Pettit, & Fischoff, 1969).

Nonorganic failure to thrive is probably not due solely to a lack of calories or a lack of affection. There are also likely to be other factors within the child, as well as defects in the interaction between the child and parents which, when added to a combination of poor caloric intake and insufficient affection and stimulation, become responsible for the condition. Nonorganic failure to thrive, better described as growth failure in infants secondary to a dysfunction of the maternal–child interaction, is a complex problem involving not only caloric intake but also the availability of parental, physical, and emotional resources for the infants, as well as the infant's ability to respond to these resources.

Family Characteristics

A variety of characteristics have been described in the families of these infants and in the infants themselves. Sometimes, the parents have unusual beliefs or perceptions about what constitutes a normal diet for an infant. More often, there is a distorted mother–infant relationship.

There are often multiple problems within the family, including poverty, overcrowding, unemployment, illegitimacy, and seriously disturbed marital relationships. The mothers are reported to be lonely and isolated and the fathers are often absent, uninvolved in family life, and unsupportive. Maternal depression and suicide attempts sometimes occur, and there is often a common theme of profound emotional and physical deprivation in the mother's own early childhood. The parents may have little to spare from their own meager stores of affection to pass on to their offspring (Togut, Allen, & Lelchuck, 1969). Although most of the families described in the scientific literature have come from low socioeconomic groups, the condition is also seen in stable, intact families in favorable economic circumstances.

As these families have a spectrum of problems, it is helpful to try to categorize them so as to be able to plan treatment. Kempe, Cutler, & Dean (1980) described three groups of mothers, each requiring a different approach. In one group, the mothers are basically capable, but are overwhelmed by external problems. This group is likely to respond to help aimed at relieving some of the external stresses. The second group contains mothers who are immature, chronically deprived, and depressed. They may have had no good role model in their own childhood and have few emotional resources to spare for their infant. They require more intensive treatment, combining practical assessment with therapy aimed at helping them to understand the needs of their infant. The third group, where treatment is likely to be more difficult and where separation may be required, comprises parents who are antisocial and aggressive or who have a distorted image of their infant, often regarding the child as bad and denying that there is a feeding problem or that any help is needed.

Some of the families have a number of features similar to those seen in families where physical abuse occurs, such as the parents' own childhood experience of neglect or abuse, lack of family support, and parental attitudes toward the infant. A continuum between growth failure in infancy and later physical abuse has been described, with two children out of a series of 24 initially assessed for nonorganic failure to thrive later dying as a result of injuries inflicted by their parents or caretakers and three others suffering suspicious, nonfatal injuries (Oates, 1985).

Infant Characteristics

A number of characteristics of these infants have been noted although it is not always clear whether these are primary or secondary. The infants have been described as being fussier, more demanding, and unsociable, less adaptable, more inconsolable, and less happy than normal controls. They are often below average in their development, have immature or abnormal oral-motor skills, making them more difficult to feed, and have more negative affect in feeding than seen in other infants. These two vignettes illustrate some of the variations seen in this condition.

Jessica was brought to the emergency room of a hospital when she was 16 months old. Her mother, Julie, complained that there was a fever and that Jessica was listless. Although the physical examination showed only a simple upper respiratory tract infection, the staff was concerned about her low weight, which was well below the third percentile for a child of her age. Jessica was unkempt, and had loss of subcutaneous fat, and marked muscle wasting. Her development was at an 11-month level. There were also bruises on the buttocks and abdomen, suggesting physical abuse.

Jessica was Julie's fifth child, the eldest two now living in foster care. Julie was of limited intelligence and was currently living with a man she feared because of his violent outbursts. Julie seemed to be unaware of her child's small size and thinness. Her own childhood had been one of deprivation and

emotional neglect, leaving her with few inner resources to care for her own children.

Jessica was admitted to the hospital, where she ate
ravenously. Her weight rapidly improved and she
started to make developmental progress. Further
family assessment led to a serious concern about
Julie's ability to adequately care for her daughter.
Jessica was placed with a caring foster family where
she continued to progress in growth and development. Julie was assisted with family planning and
with supportive community resources to help her
adequately care for her other children.

Luke was Sue and Gary's first child and they were
extremely proud of him. Sue gave up her job as a
beauty consultant to care for him, confident that
Gary's income as an accountant would be adequate for
their needs. She decided not to breast-feed in the hope
that her figure would be preserved.

Luke was not an easy baby. He had mild gastroe-
sophageal reflux, often bringing up small amounts of
sour-smelling milk after a feeding and crying with the
discomfort. Sue, who liked things to be clean and
tidy, did not enjoy feeding him. She found that if she
gave him smaller amounts of food, the problem of
reflux was less, and, as he slept well, she found it more
convenient to let him sleep through some of his
feeding times. Sue was also influenced by a friend
who frequently advised her about how best to feed
Luke, based on her reading and interest in alternative
medicine. She had encouraged Sue, who was a
receptive listener, to prevent Luke from becoming fat,
saying that this would have bad consequences for his
future.

When he was almost 4 months old, Luke developed a fever and was taken to the family physician.
A middle ear infection was found and treated, although what concerned the doctor more was Luke's

size and appearance. Luke weighed a little less than he had at the time he was born. He had loss of muscle bulk and fat. There was little spontaneous smiling or vocalization.

It became clear from talks with Sue that the problem was one of underfeeding. Luke and his parents were referred to a growth clinic where they were seen by a social worker, nurse, pediatrician, and nutritionist. A plan was instituted to provide adequate nutrition and to help the parents respond more appropriately to Luke's needs. Weekly appointments were made. Considerable emphasis was placed on understanding the parents' views of Luke's needs and reeducating them about more appropriate ways of feeding him. Luke gained weight quickly with this plan and started smiling and vocalizing more often. As Luke and his parents made progress, the frequency of the visits was diminished, although arrangements were made to see them intermittently over the next two years.

An Approach to the Assessment and Management in Nonorganic Failure to Thrive

The diagnosis of nonorganic failure to thrive can usually be made by the taking of a careful history from the parents and examination of the child. Because a variety of medical problems can cause growth failure, an assessment by a pediatric physician is essential. The pediatrician will usually be able to make the diagnosis on the basis of the story and the physical examination. Laboratory investigations are only occasionally helpful.

Where possible, the parent and child should be together while the information about the child and family is being obtained, as this is an ideal opportunity to observe the parent–child interaction. It is important that the information be obtained in a way that is nonjudgmental so that the parents will feel like partners in trying to find the cause for the child's growth failure. Inquiries about the child's birthweight, previous growth pattern, and general health should be made. Particular emphasis should be placed on the child's feeding behavior and intake. Specific questions are needed to be able to calculate the daily intake and compare this with the child's nutritional needs based on age and expected weight for this age. Observing the mother feeding the child, something that can be done during the interview, provides valuable information about the feeding technique, how the mother relates to the child, and the infant's feeding behavior.

It is helpful to gain an understanding of what the parent believes to be the problem and what the parent thinks is necessary for the infant's adequate nutrition, as well as tracing the source of these parental beliefs. Some parents are just following bad advice from a well-meaning but misguided friend or relative, whereas others may have an abnormal perception of the child's needs.

One can obtain useful information by going through a typical day with the parent, starting with the time the infant wakes, asking who in the family responds to the infant's needs, who does the feeding, who also is responsible for sharing the care of the infant, whether the infant is often left alone, and whether the mother has any sense of enjoyment from being with her infant.

Information about the infant's growth and development should include previous weight records, if available, and information about developmental milestones, since many infants with nonorganic failure to thrive have developmental delays. Lack of parental awareness about developmental milestones would be a cause for concern.

Psychosocial inquiries should look at the parents' own childhood backgrounds, their current emotional supports, their beliefs about correct childrearing, and the source of these beliefs. It is particularly helpful to ask about their expectations for the infant. If the infant lives with both parents, they should both participate in this interview where possible.

Physical Findings

When the infant is medically examined, there should be an inspection for any marks, such as bruising, that might suggest concurrent physical abuse. These children may appear to have relatively large heads in relation to their body, although this is an illusion caused by the fact that the body is wasted, the face is often thin and anxious looking, and there is loss of muscle size and subcutaneous fat. This loss of muscle and fat is most noticeable at the buttocks and thighs where loose folds of skin may be seen.

Some unusual behaviors may be noted. The infant may adopt a posture more typical of a younger infant when lying in bed and the legs may remain flexed at the hips when an attempt is made to hold the infant in a standing position. Some malnourished and deprived children exhibit self-stimulatory rhythmic behavior, such as head banging, body rocking, or rumination. A delay in developmental milestones may be found on developmental assessment. Some of these infants will be irritable and difficult to comfort. Others are withdrawn, avoid eye contact, and do not smile.

Management

Management involves addressing the relationship and attachment problems in the family, as well as providing the infant with enough calories to reach and maintain normal weight for age. The aims of management should be:

1. To correct the malnutrition and commence catch-up growth.
2. To provide an atmosphere where the infant's development also improves.
3. To involve the parents in the management, except in those cases where it has already been decided that the child cannot be returned to the family.

Management often involves a team approach that includes a nutritionist, social worker, psychologist or psychiatrist, pediatrician, and child protection case worker. Sometimes, a brief hospital admission is required, although the infant can usually be managed through regular clinic visits. Linking the child with a growth and nutrition clinic that has an understanding of nonorganic failure to thrive can be valuable. Visits should be regular and frequent, with emphasis on supporting the parents in developing an understanding of the infant's needs and congratulating them as feeding and developmental gains take place. For parents who are unable to respond to this approach, there may need to be intervention from a child protection service. Obviously, when the growth failure clearly appears to have been due to neglect, notification of the relevant agency should be made.

Once the goal of expected weight for age has been reached and satisfactory growth is continuing, visits may be less frequent, although it is important to emphasize that this is a long-term problem, requiring ongoing review.

Along with the feeding program, the child should be receiving developmental stimulation. This will be based on the infant's needs as determined by the developmental assessment. For the nutritional and the developmental programs, the mother should be seen as the infant's main provider and caretaker, with the professional team providing assistance so that the mother can be helped to achieve the treatment goals. As many parents of these infants are not confident in their parenting abilities, it is important for those professionals involved in the case to be encouraging and to give the mother credit for her infant's progress.

Some parents are easier to help than others. When one is assessing parental competence, the parents' sensitivity to their infant's needs and developing ability should be considered. There are also other factors that influence parental competence, such as their own inner resources (partly dependent on their early developmental experiences); the characteristics of the child, including tempera-

ment, physical health, illness, age, and sex; the parents'
own relationships, their family and social network, their
employment, and their ability to use other community
resources. These factors need to be considered when one
is working with the parents toward optimum nutritional,
intellectual, and emotional development for the infant.

We now understand that nonorganic failure to thrive is
a complex problem and does not have a simple answer. It
is not just a matter of more food or more stimulation, nor
is it solely a matter of focusing on maternal factors. Each
family should be assessed individually, so as to identify
strengths and weaknesses, which interact with each other
and that can be utilized and compensated for in management.

While there will be common threads in these families,
each will have a distinctive profile. In some cases, the
child's behavior may be a major factor, whereas in others
external stresses may be predominant. In some, it may be
maternal skills that need enhancement, and in others,
deep-seated problems in the parents' own past may have to
be resolved. All of these family factors of parental background, personality, and stresses, as well as the child
factors, interact with each other. In some families, simple,
practical measures may be sufficient, but in others removal
of the child may be the option that proves in the child's best
interests.

What is important in many of these cases is that the
problems in the family that led to the growth failure are
long-term ones that require ongoing attention. Even though
the child may recover from the growth problem, the underlying family problems may continue to affect the child's
behavior and personality development. This is why many
of these families need much more than a thorough initial
assessment and a management plan. They also need regular review and modification of the management plan, as
well as specific help for the child in the development of
acceptable behavior and personality characteristics.

6

WHAT HAPPENS
TO ABUSED CHILDREN?

Much is known about the characteristics of families in which child abuse occurs and about the various injuries and behaviors of abused children. Less is known about the long-term consequences of abuse. The area that is best researched, largely because of several good population studies, is sexual abuse, the most recently recognized area in the spectrum of child abuse. This chapter will discuss some of the studies, looking at the consequences of physical abuse, neglect (including failure to thrive), and sexual abuse.

It is important to know what happens to these children in the long term because this information can be used for planning and modifying services. Such information will enable judgments to be made about which therapeutic or protective programs initiated at the time of recognition have been successful, which family characteristics are likely to be associated with a poor outcome, and which children are likely to do well. Such data could aid in decisions about appropriate and inappropriate treatment programs, the value of alternate placement, the length of such placement, and the length and time of treatment likely to be associated with the best outcome.

PHYSICAL ABUSE

Elmer and Gregg in 1967 were among the first to describe the high degree of neurological, developmental, and psychological disabilities suffered by physically abused children. They reviewed 20 children out of an original group of 50 at an average of five years after the abuse. Forty percent of these children were found to be emotionally disturbed and half had IQ scores below 80. When 25 physically abused children were reassessed after three years by Morse, Sahler, & Friedman (1970), nine were described as being mentally retarded, six were emotionally disturbed, and 15 were regarded as "problems" by their parents. Similar findings were reported by Martin (1972) in a three-year follow-up of 42 children: one third of these children had an IQ below 80 and over one third had language delay. A review of 50 abused children, some of whom only had mild injury, found that even though IQ was not a major problem, the median IQ of the group being 98, there were a variety of personality and neurological difficulties. Sixty percent had an impaired capacity to enjoy life, 62% had behavioral problems, 62% had low self-esteem, and 30% had significant neurological impairment (Martin & Beezley, 1977).

A problem with these studies is that they had relatively small samples and lacked a control group. It could be argued that, as much of the detected physical abuse is in lower socioeconomic groups and multiple-problem families, some of the problems found in these children may have been a product of social class and other family problems, such as alcohol or drug difficulties, which could be more powerful influences on subsequent development than the abuse.

Control studies to try to disentangle the effects of these factors from the effect of the abuse suggest that there still seems to be a problem in the medium to long term even after allowing for these variables.

Lynch and Roberts (1982) allowed for family variables by including siblings as controls in a 4-year follow-up of 30 physically abused children. At follow-up, there were problems in the siblings, as well as in the abused children, although not as marked. Forty-one percent of the abused children and 28% of their siblings had IQ scores of less than 90. Language delay was more marked in the abused children, occurring in 36% compared with 28% of the siblings.

One of the first prospective studies that looked at the developmental consequences of different patterns of mal-treatment was carried out by Egeland et al. in 1983. These researchers followed 267 high-risk families for four years and looked at the characteristics of the children in relation to the pattern of maltreatment that had taken place. The four different patterns of maltreatment initially defined were (1) physical abuse, (2) hostility and verbal abuse, (3) parents who were psychologically unavailable, and (4) parents who were neglectful. It was found that when these children were observed in a preschool situation, the physi-cally abused children were distractible, and lacked persis-tence, ego control, and enthusiasm. They also experienced considerable negative emotions. Those children whose mothers were psychologically unavailable showed a marked increase in maladaptive patterns of functioning. The children who had been neglected were found to have considerable difficulty in dealing with the various tasks acquired in the preschool situation because they lacked self-esteem.

This study was useful in helping to emphasize that child abuse and neglect cover a wide range of behaviors, with the outcomes depending partly on family characteristics, as well as on the actual abuse. Information such as this highlights the need for careful, thorough assessment in each case. Such an assessment needs to include the child as well as the parents so that a specific treatment plan can be made that takes into account the child's particular needs.

When 39 of 56 children originally seen at the Camper-down Children's Hospital in Sydney were reviewed five to six years after the diagnosis of physical abuse and the pattern of intelligence was compared with a control group matched for age, sex, ethnic background and social class, the children were found to have problems consistent with earlier studies.

The abused children had significantly lower verbal and performance IQ scores than the controls (95 compared with 106). Eight of these abused children had suffered head injuries. The mean IQ of this subgroup was 90, not enough to account for the IQ difference between the abused children and the controls. These children were also significantly behind the controls in language development and reading skills. The abused group had an average of 14 months reading delay for age compared with a five-month delay in the controls.

The abused children also had lower self-esteem and were more likely than the controls to be serious, cautious, and subdued on personality testing, in contrast to the controls, who were more socially outgoing. When the teachers of these children, who were unaware of the history of abuse, were asked to complete a behavior questionnaire designed for teachers (Rutter, 1967), 55% of the abused children received an abnormal score, predominantly in the antisocial range. This compared with 18% of controls receiving an abnormal score. When the mothers completed a similar behavior questionnaire on their own children, 81% of the mothers who had abused their children gave their children an abnormal score, compared with 35% of controls.

The only area where there was no difference between these two groups of children was on a social maturity scale where the abused and comparison children had similar scores. This may be because these abused children, since they were often left to fend for themselves, had to become adept at some of the skills that the maturity scale measured (Oates, Peacock, & Forrest, 1984).

A problem with all of these studies is that, even though they contain control groups, the numbers are quite small and the length of follow-up is relatively short. More recent follow-up studies have contained larger numbers and some have had follow-up into adult life. Nineteen of the 50 severely abused children in the 1967 study of Elmer and Gregg were followed into adult life (Martin & Elmer, 1992). Six adults had completed some college education and six had not completed high school. Five showed evidence of intellectual retardation, although this is not surprising as central nervous system damage had been documented in some cases in the original study. Those the study was not able to follow up on had had more problems on their initial childhood assessment, suggesting that it was the better functioning group that could be traced for the long-term review.

Three large-scale studies confirmed the problems of poor intellectual performance in physically abused children. When 139 abused and nonabused school-age children and adults were reviewed in an analysis that controlled for socioeconomic status, the abused children were more likely to have repeated a grade at school and had overall poorer school performance than the nonabused group (Wodarski, Kurtz, Gaudin, & Howing, 1990). The longest-term and largest follow-up study (Perez & Widom, 1994) reviewed 413 abused and neglected children in their adult life at an average age of 28 years. These adults tested significantly lower in their IQ scores and reading ability than controls, even after the analysis controlled for economic status and other variables.

It is clear that physical abuse has long-term adverse outcomes, particularly on intellectual functioning, language and reading skills, and probably on personality development. What is not clear is why this occurs. As bruising is the most common injury seen in physical abuse and as the majority of abused children do not suffer from head injury, it is difficult to argue that these problems are a direct result of head injury. It is likely that it is the family environment in which many of these children remain (an environment that may continue to be abusive, neglectful, and understimulating) that produces these long-term consequences. This suggests an avenue for future research where the long-term development of physically abused children who remained with their families could be compared with that of children who were brought up in more suitable environments following the abuse, taking into account the amount and type of treatment given.

Another possibility is that the abusive event or events altered the children's personality and behavior so that they became less available for teaching and learning. Or it may be that some of these children had developmental delay before the abuse occurred, making them more difficult to manage and putting them at greater risk of being abused.

NEGLECT AND NONORGANIC FAILURE TO THRIVE

In children with nonorganic failure to thrive, the two questions that arise are: Do the children catch up in their growth? Are there any long-term intellectual defects? The majority of follow-up studies show that there is catch-up growth, although a 13-year follow-up found that, while all of the failure-to-thrive children were by then in the normal range for weight and height, they were significantly more likely to be smaller and lighter than controls when weight for age was compared (Oates, Peacock, & Forrest, 1985).

There have been few long-term studies looking at outcome in nonorganic failure to thrive. Shorter-term studies have shown behavior difficulties in almost 50% (Elmer, Gregg, & Ellison, 1969) and a high incidence of developmental delay (Haynes et al., 1984). A 13-year follow-up using a control group matched for social class and ethnic background (Oates et al., 1985) found verbal language skills to be a major defect. Although the study and control groups were not different overall on their IQ scores, the group that had failed to thrive had lower verbal IQ scores than did controls. They were also behind controls on other measures of verbal ability and in their reading skills. In contrast to follow-up studies of abused children, there were no differences between self-esteem scores in the failure-to-thrive group and the controls.

Problems found at long-term follow-up in children with non-organic failure to thrive raise the question as to whether it was the malnutrition in infancy that led to these ongoing cognitive problems or whether the problems were a result of some pre-existing problem in the children or in their family environments. The relationship between early malnutrition and intellectual functioning is complex as factors other than the malnutrition have to be considered, including the timing of the malnutrition, the presence of coexistent disease, economic status, and the stability of the family. These factors probably explain the conflicting results of studies. For example, Galler, Ramsey, and Forde (1985) found that infants who suffered moderate to severe malnutrition had lower IQs than controls four years later, but Richardson (1976) showed that malnourished children with a favorable social background had an average IQ score only two points lower than controls, whereas those from an unfavorable background had an average IQ nine points lower than controls.

Although failure to thrive has been followed up separately from physical abuse in several studies, it is more difficult to obtain information on what happens to children who were neglected but not physically abused. This is because neglected and physically abused children are usually included in the same group in most studies and rarely looked at separately. A recent study (Eckenrode, Laird, & Doris, 1995) that analyzed the results for neglected and physically abused children separately found that the neglected children had poorer school performance than the physically abused children, even after accounting for social class. This finding adds further support to the view that it is not the physical injury so much as other family, emotional, and environmental factors that account for these ongoing problems.

SEXUAL ABUSE

As child sexual abuse is now known to be common, it is important to look at what evidence there is that it has an adverse outcome. A problem with most outcome studies is that they have not distinguished between the many different types of child sexual abuse. There are a number of factors that may affect outcome, including the type of abuse (whether achieved by force, coercion, bribery, or uninformed consent); the age and maturity of the child when the abuse occurred; whether the abuse was an isolated episode or it had been ongoing over a long period; the relationship between the offender and the victim; and the age difference between the parties. Other factors that may affect outcome are the nature and extent of the sexual contact, such as intercourse, genital manipulation, or exhibitionism, and whether the abuse was recognized, and, if so, the nature of treatment provided. In cases of intrafamilial abuse, information as to whether the offender remains in the home following disclosure has to be considered, as well as underlying strengths and weaknesses in the child's family.

Apart from the problems of not distinguishing among the different types and extent of abuse, most outcome studies have additional problems in their methodology. Many of the reported series are biased because they come from clinical populations where the abused subjects have presented for treatment because of problems. Some studies have not used control groups, many do not use standardized outcome measures, others group males and females together, and many do not look at the presence of other family problems. As sexual abuse often occurs in the presence of multiple family problems, it is difficult to sift out what proportion of any disturbance found is due to sexual abuse and what proportion may be due to other problems in the family.

Finally, there are some areas on which future research should place more emphasis. A great deal more study needs to be done on the characteristics of families in which child sexual abuse has occurred. The study of perpetrators of child sexual abuse has not been looked at as widely as studies of the victims and, perhaps most important, little attention has been paid to the strengths in children and families that may allow some children to be less disturbed than others following sexual abuse.

Early Studies on Child Sexual Abuse

The earlier studies reflect most of the above problems, whereas more recent studies, being more sophisticated in their design, are more likely to be accurate. Before the 1970s, clinicians held diverse views on the effects of child sexual abuse, some suggesting that it had little impact. Kinsey and colleagues (1953) concluded that this type of sexual activity could contribute favorably to psychosexual development. Others suggested that sexual abuse had only minimal effects on children's psychological development (Gagnon, 1965) and that children who had been involved in incestuous relationships with their parents were not severely damaged (Yorukoglu & Kemph, 1966).

A study by Burton (1968) of 41 children who had been sexually abused concluded that there was little evidence of detrimental effects on their subsequent personality development when they were reviewed between one and seven years after the assault. The only effect found was a significant difference in affection-seeking behavior between the abused and the control children. One problem with this study is that the major test used was projective, easily open to interpretation, and it was given and analyzed by the investigator, who was not blinded as to which children were in the study and control groups.

One of the early studies that did show a high degree of adverse sequelae was by De Francis (1969), who found that 66% of the 250 sexually abused children he studied were emotionally disturbed by the abuse, 52% being mildly to moderately disturbed and 14% being seriously disturbed.

However, as all subjects in this study came from lower socioeconomic groups and had multiple other problems, it is likely that a proportion of the problems found were due to factors in these families that were in addition to the sexual abuse.

Short-Term Effects of Child Sexual Abuse

In an evaluation of 45 sexually abused children (average age 5.3 years) over an 18-month period and seen within two months of the diagnosis, 31% of the children were found to be free from psychological symptoms, but over two thirds had one or more problems (Mannarino & Cohen, 1986), the most common of which were nightmares, bed-wetting, sadness, clinging behavior, anxiety, and inappropriate sexual behavior. No control group was used in this study.

The Achenbach Child Behavior Checklist was used by Friedrich and colleagues (1986) to look for disturbance in a study of 85 children between the ages of 3 and 12 years who had been sexually abused within the preceding two years. It was found that over 35% of the sample had significant abnormalities on the Achenbach profile, much higher than would be expected in a normal population. This study also showed, as many working in this area have suspected, that the degree of disturbance increased with the increasing invasiveness of the abuse, with the closeness of the relationship between the perpetrator and the child, and with the duration and frequency of the abuse.

A study from Tufts University (1984) looked at the degree of disturbance in children from two different age groups. In this study, 156 male and female children were seen where the diagnosis of sexual abuse had been made in the previous six months. It was found that 17% of the younger children—between 4 and 6 years old—had clinically significant pathology, showing more aggressive and anti-social behavior than expected on the norms for the tests used. Twenty-seven percent of the children in this age group scored significantly above general population norms on a sexual behavior scale that included such items as open masturbation, excessive sexual curiosity, and frequent exposure of the genitals.

A controlled study (Tong, Oates, & McDowell, 1987) of 37 girls and 12 boys who had been sexually abused on an average of 2.6 years previously found that on the Achenbach Child Behavior Checklist a significantly higher proportion of the abused children fell outside the normal range compared with the controls. The sexually abused children also had significantly lower self-esteem than the controls. Interviews with the nonoffending parents of these children showed that 76% of the children were thought to be less confident than before the abuse. Thirty percent were reported as having fewer friends and 20% were said to be aggressive.

Deterioration in school performance may follow sexual abuse, although the effect on school abilities does not appear to be as clear as for physical abuse and neglect. When Eckenrode et al. (1995) compared school performance among neglected, physically abused, and sexually abused children and controls, in contrast to the physically abused and neglected children, who performed more poorly, the sexually abused children did not differ from the comparison group in reading and math scores. This finding appears to persist into adult life as a study of adults abused in their childhood showed that, while the physically abused children continued to have reading problems and had lower IQ scores, the adults who were sexually abused as children were not different from controls in this area.

As well as having an increased level of inappropriate sexual behavior and psychological symptoms, sexually abused children appear to be at increased risk of later criminal activity. A study of 107 children aged 14 or older, who were sexually abused at an average of 2.6 years previously, were traced through police files that record crimes committed by individuals over the age of 14 years old. The point of the study was to determine whether any of the abused children had been convicted of crimes during the period between the episode of sexual abuse and this review. It was found that five (21%) of the 24 boys and five (6%) of the 83 girls had been convicted of a crime since they had been sexually abused. This compared with a 2.6% prevalence of criminal convictions in boys aged 14 to 19 years and a 0.7% prevalence of criminal convictions for girls in this age range. All of the crimes took the form of either robbery or assault, suggesting that for this group sexual assault left a strong residue of anger and deprivation that later manifested as violent behavior and robbery (Oates & Tong, 1987).

This increased risk of criminal behavior appears to be long-lasting, with much of the behavior being in the sexual area. A recent study using a large sample (Widom & Ames, 1994) found that, compared with other types of abuse and neglect, early childhood sexual abuse did not increase a person's risk for later adult and delinquent behavior compared with children who suffered other types of abuse and neglect. As adults, child sexual abuse victims were at higher risk of arrest for sex crimes than controls. This finding was also true for victims of physical abuse and neglect.

Although much of the information on the effects of child sexual abuse is on older children, a variety of effects have been described in preschool children who are sexually abused. That children feel guilty for the sexual abuse is common. They tend to blame themselves for the abuse and feel especially guilty if they enjoy aspects of it. Although preschoolers often do not experience this guilt in the short-term, typically it has been found to become a problem for them as they grow older (Lusk & Waterman, 1986).

Anxiety, which can be quite severe, has been documented in preschool children. A study by Adams-Tucker (1982), which included preschoolers, showed that anxiety was a major presenting problem that could become manifest as behavioral symptoms, phobias, nightmares, and separation anxiety. Along with the anxiety, extreme levels of fear have been noted in sexually abused preschoolers. This fear can follow shortly after the abuse itself, such as fear of adults or fear of what will happen in the future, or it can be manifested as phobias later in life.

Studies have shown depression and anger to be frequent reactions among preschoolers who have been sexually abused. The anger is commonly directed toward the parents. Psychosomatic complaints have been noted in sexually abused preschool children, including stomachaches, headaches, hypochondriasis, fecal soiling, bed-wetting, and excessive blinking (Adams-Tucker, 1982).

One of the most useful studies on child sexual abuse in preschool children is that of Finkelhor and colleagues (1988c). This study provided information on 87 children sexually abused in preschool, with an in-depth study of 43 of these cases. It showed that nursery preschool children abused in a day-care setting can have a broad range of symptoms.

The most commonly mentioned reaction in this study was fear, occurring in 69 of 87 cases. The fear took many forms, including fear of going to day care, fear of being left alone, and fear of real or imagined objects or persons. The fears could range from the ordinary to the bizarre. At times, the fears persisted beyond the normal time period when one can accept unusual fears of this age group and were so extreme that the children were immobilized by them.

The second most common disturbance was nightmares and sleep disturbances, occurring in 68 of 87 cases. Eighty-seven percent of children under 3 years old experienced problems with nightmares and night terrors. Fifty-three percent of these children had clinging behavior, needing continual reassurance from their parents after the abuse occurred. It was not uncommon for a parent to have to stay at home with a child for a period of time after the abuse was discovered.

Inappropriate sexual behavior—excessive masturbation, simulated sexual acts with siblings or friends, precocious or flirtatious behavior, unusual sexual knowledge for the

child's age and development, sexualized kissing in relationship with parents and friends, and compulsive sexual
behavior such as grabbing breasts or genitals—was experienced by 46% of the children in this study. Other common
symptoms included bed-wetting (36%) and aggressive
behavior (32%). Twenty-nine percent of children developed a distrust of adults. Twenty-six percent had difficulties in play and relationships with other children, while
25% had a problem with tantrums following the abuse.

The study looked at family factors and the type of abuse
to see if there were relationships between these factors and
the symptoms. It was found that only one child had no
psychological symptoms in the period following sexual
abuse. The analysis showed some expected relationships,
such as the fact that children with poor quality parenting,
those who were more forcibly abused, those who were
penetrated sexually, and those for whom there was a long
period between the abuse and its disclosure had a greater
number of symptoms.

It was also found that one of the major factors relating to
symptoms was the relationship of the child to the perpetrator. If one of the perpetrators was a child care worker or a
preschool worker (as opposed to an outsider or preschool
maintenance person), then the child was likely to experience a greater number of symptoms regardless of whether
the case involved force, penetration or ritualistic abuse and
regardless of the quality of parenting. Burns and colleagues
(1988) concluded that abuse by the person responsible for
giving care seemed to violate a child's sense of trust, safety,
and security more, leaving the child with a more profound
sense of betrayal. Abuse by someone close to the child is
also likely to create the fear that other trusted adults could
be abusive.

Other factors relating to a higher number of abnormal
symptoms included the use of force and the involvement
of ritualistic abuse. The children who were subjected to
ritualistic abuse had increased numbers of symptoms, no
matter how much force or what kinds of sexual acts were

involved. Symptoms were also more likely in children whose mothers had a significant impairment in their child-rearing skills, such as alcoholism, drug addiction, mental illness, or other problems that interfered with functioning as a mother.

While it is clear from these studies that sexually abused children experience a number of disturbances, at least in the short term, and although there is some consistency among the symptoms, none of these features can be used to confirm that sexual abuse has occurred. The presence of such disturbances, however, should lead to sexual abuse being considered as one of the possible causes. Probably more important than the actual physical details of abuse is the emotional aspect of abuse, including the threats and the fear that are part of it. As would be expected, the more invasive forms of abuse seem to have more sequelae, with a recent study showing no adverse effects of noncontact sexual abuse (such as sexual requests and exhibitionism) in men on a long-term follow-up, but persisting features of psychological dysfunctioning in men who had suffered child sexual abuse involving physical sexual contact (Collings, 1995).

It is sometimes assumed that intrafamilial abuse has more serious effects than extrafamilial abuse. However, a prospective, controlled study of 84 sexually abused children seen at the time of diagnosis and reviewed 18 months later found no correlation between adverse outcome and the relationship of the offender to the child. More important factors were the supportiveness of the child's mother and the stability of family function, both of which made an adverse outcome less likely (Oates et al., 1994; Stern et al., 1995).

Long-Term Effects of Child Sexual Abuse

There is now increasing evidence to support the view that a significant number of child victims have problems in adult life, including depressive symptoms, sexual disorders, anxiety, low self-esteem, a tendency to revictimization, self-destructive behavior, and drug or alcohol abuse. Most of the good long-term studies on the effects of child sexual abuse come from populations of adults, the best being from random population studies. The basic design is that a random population of adults is selected and the subjects are interviewed or asked to anonymously complete some questions or psychological measures, which might include indices of depression, self-esteem, alcohol and drug use, as well as sexual and other behaviors. The survey instrument also asks about any childhood experience of sexual abuse. This information then allows the researchers to divide the responses into two broad groups, those who were sexually abused as children and those who were not. These two groups can then be compared on the basis of their responses to the other questions. A number of good studies on adult populations have been performed. It is probably time that the long-term effects of child physical and emotional abuse were studied in this way.

Depression has been shown in two population studies. Briere and Runtz (1988) studied 278 undergraduate college females and found that those who recalled sexual abuse in childhood experienced more depressive symptoms than did nonabused controls. This group of young adults also had a significantly greater number of nightmares, anxiety attacks, and sleep disturbances than the nonabused controls. A similar high incidence of depression was found in 301 female college students, where 65% of those who recalled sexual abuse in their childhood recorded symptoms of depression compared with 43% of controls (Sedney & Brooks, 1984). Eighteen percent of the sexually abused group in this study had been hospitalized for depression. This study also showed that 30% of the abused sample reported having thoughts of wanting to hurt themselves compared with 16% of controls. In the abuse group, 16% had made at least one suicide attempt, compared with 6% of controls.

Findings such as this, based on college populations,

have been supported by random population studies. A random sample of 119 Los Angeles women found that in those cases where there had been sexual abuse involving physical contact, there was a higher incidence of depression than in the normal population after family background factors had been controlled for (Peters, 1988). Bagley and Ramsay (1986) used a random sample of 387 adult women and showed that 17% of those who had suffered from childhood sexual abuse had symptoms of depression compared with 9% of controls. Low self-esteem was noted in 19% of these women compared with 5% in the controls.

These findings were similar in a New Zealand study, which used a random community sample to look at the relationship between women's mental health and their past experiences of sexual abuse. Twenty percent of women who had been exposed to sexual abuse as children were identified as having psychiatric symptoms that were predominantly depressive in type compared with 6.3% of the nonabused population, suggesting that the effects of abuse contribute to psychiatric morbidity for many years after the event (Mullen, Romans-Clarkson, Walton, & Herbison, 1988).

Child sexual abuse has also been associated with later self-destructive behavior and drug or alcohol abuse. Peters (1988) found that 17% of women who had experienced child sexual abuse now had symptoms of alcohol abuse, compared with 4% of nonabused. Briere and Runtz (1988) found that 27% of child sexual abuse victims had a history of alcoholism in adult life compared with 11% of nonvictims, whereas 21% of those who had been abused had a history of drug addiction compared with 2% of nonvictims.

Finkelhor (1984) compared 121 male and female college students who had been sexually abused in childhood with 685 students who had not been abused and controlled for family variables in the analysis. He found that sexual self-esteem was low in the males and females who had been abused as children. The study controlled for all of the background factors that could have influenced sexual self-esteem—such as social class, ethnic background, family size, family values, parental attitudes, and education—and found that the relationship still held. It also showed that for males there was a connection between childhood sexual abuse and adult homosexual activity. Boys victimized by older men were over four times more likely to be engaged in homosexual activity at the time of the survey than those who had not been abused. No such relationship was noted for girls.

It is clear that despite methodological differences most studies on child sexual abuse show that a significant proportion of children have effects in the short term and that these effects often continue into adult life. Not all children show both short- and long-term adverse effects. This may reflect a problem with the measures used. It may be related to ameliorating influences, such as the availability of other supportive members in the family, or it may be because of the inner resilience of some children. These areas require further investigation. Similarly, less research has been done on the effects of sexual abuse on boys than on the effects on girls, although the evidence strongly indicates that a significant proportion of boys also have adverse long-term effects.

In adult life, almost half of the victims, depending on the study, do not show any disturbance on the measures used. This is comforting information to give to families, although it is not possible at this stage to know which children are likely to have long-term effects and which are not. It would be unfortunate if, in the desire to be aware of the later effects of child sexual abuse, one forgot the impact of the event on childhood itself. This has been succinctly stated by Browne and Finkelhor (1986).

> Effects seem to be considered less serious if the impact is transient and disappears in the course of development. However this tendency to assess everything in

terms of its long-term effects betrays an "adultocentric" bias. Adult traumas such as rape are not assessed ultimately in terms of whether or not they will have an impact on old age. They are acknowledged to be painful and alarming events whether their impact lasts for one year or ten. Similarly, childhood trauma should not be dismissed because no "long-term effects" can be demonstrated. Child sexual abuse needs to be recognized as a serious problem of childhood if only for the immediate pain, confusion and upset that can ensue. (p. 178)

The challenge with all forms of child abuse is to aim for effective prevention programs and adequate treatment. Because the problem is so large and the resources, though sometimes considerable, are still relatively small in relation to the size of the problem, there will never be enough resources to provide adequate treatment for all children. Two conclusions can be drawn from this. The first is that there need to be ways to treat these problems effectively and to develop methods of evaluating treatment so as to measure failure as well as success. This will at least allow limited treatment resources to be used effectively and will also allow other treatment methods to be abandoned, painful as this may be, if they are found to ineffective. The second conclusion is that more emphasis needs to be placed on early intervention and prevention, emphasis that may mean a change in attitudes towards children, sexuality, and violence not only at a family but also at a government and community level.

7

PREVENTION

As child abuse is a very large problem involving many children, it is unlikely that there will ever be enough resources to adequately manage more than a small proportion of cases, particularly those cases that need long-term treatment. Treatment involves treating not only the abused child but also the family in which the abuse occurred. The family may need help and treatment because of the trauma that has occurred as a result of the abuse or treatment may be required because of underlying problems in the family that allowed the abuse to occur. In addition, the offender will need treatment.

As much of the response to child abuse is crisis driven, responding to what seems to be an ever-increasing number of new cases, there is often little time left for treatment, particularly when treatment is complex, involving not only the child but other family members as well. When one realizes that a parent's abusive behavior may have its roots in several years of abusive experiences when that parent was a child, it becomes clear that for some cases treatment may also need to take place over several years. Therefore, it is not surprising that, as well as a scarcity of resources for treatment, there is very little time or energy left for evaluation of effectiveness of treatment.

Evaluating treatment takes time, resources, and also courage. It takes courage to carefully evaluate one's work and to shift some of the resources that would normally be used for crisis intervention or treatment into assessing the value of treatment. It also takes courage to put one's own work "on the line," especially if evaluation shows that treatment, or some aspects of it, may not be as effective as one believed so that long-held, cherished beliefs may have to be revised. However, for the most effective use of resources, evaluation of treatment must occur.

While we have some knowledge about the value of treatment, a great deal more can be gathered. There is far less published on treating child abuse than on other aspects of abuse. A recent literature review on the treatment of physically abused children and the treatment of physically abusive adults by Oates & Bross (1995) found only 25 papers over a period of 10 years that met minimal criteria for research methodology (five or more subjects in the sample; at least 15% of the sample being physically abused, and, either pretest or posttest, a comparison group or randomization to compare the effects of treatment). Treatment duration ranged from four weeks to 12 months for parents and from four weeks to two years for children. Most programs showed some improvement with treatment, but the majority had no follow-up to see if improvement was sustained.

It may be that some families are better not treated at all. Jones (1987) suggested that families who persistently deny the abuse, refuse to accept help, have severe personality or psychiatric disorders, and where the abuse has been severe may not be able to be helped, suggesting that this should be recognized so that resources can be directed to families where the chance of success is likely to be higher.

It is also known that abuse can still occur while a family is in treatment. A review of 89 demonstration treatment programs (Cohn & Daro, 1987) found that one third or more of the parents maltreated their children while in treatment, with over half of the families being thought likely to further mistreat their children after treatment finished.

A study of 24,507 children in a child abuse and neglect registry showed that the risk of reabuse was greatest in the first year after the initial incident with reabuse occurring in over two thirds of cases. The younger the child, the greater the risk of abuse (Fryer & Miyoshi, 1994). When outcomes in terms of depression, behavior disorders, and self-esteem were looked at in sexually abused children 18 months after a diagnosis of sexual abuse was made, those who had been in treatment were no different than those who had not (Oates et al., 1994).

Such data clearly emphasize the need for a shift in direction in managing child abuse. Allocating the majority of resources to investigation, assessment, and prosecution, without providing high-quality medium- to long-term intervention for many of these children, is probably not the best way to use resources. But even before a proportion of the child abuse budget is earmarked for treatment, we need to learn more about what types of treatment are likely to be effective. This would mean that a proportion of child protection funds would need to be used for carefully designed treatment programs that compare different types of interventions and have adequate follow-up periods, preferably several years, to see whether any early response is sustained. Clearly, the treatment will depend on the underlying problem so that, as well as comparing treatment programs, the groups being treated would have to be carefully defined so that valid comparisons could be made among treatments for physically abused, neglected, emotionally abused, and sexually abused children.

Even if we are able to measure the effectiveness of treatment and have confidence, based on data, that certain treatments are effective, the reality that only a small proportion of children will be able to be helped suggests that there should be another shift in emphasis, with a greater move toward prevention.

Prevention of child abuse is likely to be cost-effective, reducing death, injury, and psychological disturbance. It should also enhance the development and subsequent parenting skills of many children who may have otherwise been at risk for perpetuating abuse in the next generation.

Preventing a proportion of abuse will also free resources for more effective management of children and families who escape the preventive net.

Just as child abuse is a complex problem, so too is prevention. Clearly multiple strategies are required. Areas that need to be addressed include societal attitudes toward the following:

- violence
- family violence
- alcohol and drug abuse
- poverty
- education of the media
- pornography
- the role of stress
- anger control
- enhancing competence and child-rearing skills of families
- public education about abuse prevention
- enhancing self-esteem of parents and children
- teaching children protective behaviors
- professional training
- treatment of abused children
- treatment of offenders
- development of family and community support networks
- parent education about child development
- treatment of parents with personality disorders

Prevention strategies also need to be based on accurate data about the characteristics of abusers and about factors that may lead them to abuse. One example of the type of data that must be considered is the finding of Fryer and Miyoshi (1994) that the risk of reabuse is higher in younger children, in females, and in the first year after the abuse, suggesting that these are areas where resources could be targeted in any tertiary prevention program. We have data about certain risk groups where abuse is more likely, so that prevention strategies could be targeted to these areas. For example, we know that physical abuse is more common in younger children, we know that children with special needs are at an increased risk of physical and sexual abuse, and we know that stress and poverty have an association with abuse.

Prevention is usually described as tertiary, secondary, or primary.

TERTIARY PREVENTION

Tertiary prevention is aimed at groups where abuse has already occurred. Although it can't prevent previous abuse, it can aim to ensure that abuse does not occur again. It is also part of good management and involves some fundamental aspects of child abuse work. These include recognition that abuse has occurred, notification of the appropriate authorities, and ensuring that the child is protected from further abuse, while at the same time taking care to see that these actions are in the best interest of the child's emotional development and that as a result of this intervention, the child does not feel punished or scapegoated. It also involves providing appropriate treatment for the child and family, as well as deciding on the most appropriate way to prevent the offender from reabusing.

An example of a tertiary prevention program is the use of a therapeutic preschool for children who have been physically and sexually abused. Such a program not only provides therapeutic day care for the children, but also involves working with the parents in helping them to develop anger control, showing them how to respond appropriately to their children's stressful behavior, and improving their own self-concept (Culpe et al., 1987; Oates et al., 1995). Although the children in a therapeutic pre-school have been abused, the aim is to prevent further abuse, to make their home environment safer for their siblings, as well as for themselves, and to provide them with skills to compensate for the trauma of their abusive environment so that they will function more effectively.

SECONDARY PREVENTION

Secondary prevention focuses on groups with a high risk of abuse occurring and tries to reduce the impact of factors that put a child at risk of being abused or a parent at risk of becoming an abuser. An example would be a program that identifies potentially abusive parents during pregnancy and provides support and resources to the identified parents with the aim of reducing the risk of abuse to the child. Another example would be providing extra re-sources for special-needs children, a group known to be at risk for sexual abuse, so that there is better supervision of the child, to reduce the risk of abuse.

It is difficult to be sure that lack of abuse means that any given preventive strategy used in a high-risk abuser group has been successful, unless it is possible to show that a similar group not engaged in the preventive program had a significantly higher rate of abuse. This can be done, as shown by Wolfe, Sandler, & Kaufman (1981). These re-searchers randomly assigned families where abuse had been documented to either a treatment group or a "wait-list." The wait-list group received the services usually provided for abuse cases, including supervision by a child welfare worker. The treatment group, however, received weekly group sessions in a clinic and concurrent home training sessions with emphasis on effective child-rearing techniques. Follow-up showed that the treatment group families were functioning more effectively in their child management skills and had no further reported episodes of abuse, 12 months after treatment.

Many secondary prevention programs have concentrated on intervention for at-risk groups during the pregnancy and perinatal period. The first well-designed study was published by Gray et al. in 1977. The at-risk group, identified during pregnancy, was composed of 100 high-risk women who were randomly assigned to either a control group that received the services usually available to abuse cases or to an intervention group. Intervention included weekly home visits by a nurse, early and more frequent follow-up contact with the pediatrician, as well as being linked with supportive services in the community. At follow-up after 35 months, five children from the control group had been hospitalized because of injuries. None of the children in the intervention group had required hospitalization. While there had been some maltreatment in both groups, children in the intervention group experienced less severe abuse than in the control group.

Some of the most comprehensive and ongoing secondary prevention programs have been reported by Olds and colleagues (1986). They initially showed that when women who were poor, young, and unmarried, and thought to be at high risk for poor caregiving, were visited regularly at home by nurses, there were fewer instances of child abuse and neglect during the first two years of life, compared with a control group that had no home visiting. The abuse rate at two years was 19% in the control group compared with 4% in the group that had the most intensive home visiting. When the children were age 2 years, the home-visited families were observed to restrict and punish their children less frequently, to provide more appropriate play materials, and to have had fewer emergency room visits during the child's first year of life (Olds, Henderson, Chamberlain, & Tatelbaum, 1986).

However, the effect on abuse reduction seemed to be lost when home visiting ceased. When the children were 4 years old, two years after the home visits had finished, no difference in the rates of child abuse or neglect were noted between the two groups, although abusive episodes in the intervention group were less serious, possibly because of earlier referral (Olds, Henderson, & Kitzman, 1994). Even though the effect on abuse was not sustained, a definite reduction had been shown in the first two years, the age when the most serious injuries are likely to occur. Those who had received home visits had other benefits that were sustained at four years. They lived in homes where there were fewer hazards, had 40% fewer injuries and accidental ingestions, had 45% fewer behavior problems, and made 35% fewer visits to emergency rooms than the high-risk, nonvisited controls. The mothers who had received intensive home visiting also had fewer subsequent pregnancies and returned to work or school more often.

While such programs appear to be effective, they are expensive and may depend to some extent on the skill and sensitivity of the nurse who is the home visitor. If volunteers could be trained and supervised to provide a similar level of effective service, costs would fall considerably. So far, there are no good published studies comparing the effectiveness of volunteer visits with professional home visiting, although one such large-scale campaign, where 750 at-risk women have been randomized into a group with no visitation, a nurse home visitation group, and a volunteer home visit group, has been started (Olds, 1993).

PRIMARY PREVENTION

Primary prevention is aimed at large segments of the population regardless of any particular risk of child abuse. A typical example would be a program to enhance parenting skills of new mothers and fathers. The thought is that by targeting a large group, those within that group who are at risk of abusive behavior will be assisted and thus the risk of abuse will be reduced. Primary preventive programs have an advantage of not stigmatizing any particular group as being "at risk." There are also helpful fringe benefits such as the value to all parents of being helped with their parenting skills. However, because large groups are involved, primary prevention programs are often expensive.

Primary prevention programs fall into three broad groups: programs aimed at professionals, programs aimed at parents, and programs aimed at children. Although child health professionals usually become involved in secondary or tertiary prevention programs, they can also have a role in providing support to families with which they are in contact, linking families with community groups and providing anticipatory guidance about child development and behavior so that parents will better understand their child's behavior.

Parents are an obvious target group for primary prevention. In contrast to physical abuse, which occurs mostly within the family, approximately 25% of sexual abuse is perpetrated by strangers and an additional 25%, approximately, is caused by people whom the child knows but who are not family members. As well, much of the intrafamilial abuse is by family members other than the parents so that parents can be in a strong position to teach their children about avoiding sexual abuse and about what to do if any sexually abusive approaches are made. This can be a valuable preventive strategy since much sexual abuse starts off slowly and gradually escalates, so that a child who has been taught about sexual abuse may be able to sound a warning in the early stages.

The use of parents in primary prevention is an area where improvements could be made as many parents do not tell their children about sexual abuse. Finkelhor (1984), in a study of 521 parents in the Boston metropolitan area, found that only 29% said that they had held discussions with their children about sexual abuse. Even when these discussions occurred, they were often not very specific. For example, in only 53% of the discussions was the possibility of abuse by an acquaintance mentioned, a figure that fell to 22% in relation to the possibility that abuse may be caused by a family member. It is understandable that parents do not wish to frighten their children unnecessarily. This fairly low figure probably also reflects the fact that, while parents are comfortable talking to their children about accidents and other potential problems, they are often uncomfortable talking with their children about sexual matters.

While much of the concern about education of parents is related to sexual abuse, they can and should also be given information about how to prevent physical abuse. This can include public education programs to which parents are exposed. Media campaigns, such as those carried out by the National Committee for the Prevention of Child Abuse, are able to send parents the message that being a parent is not easy, that everyone experiences stress in parenting at times, and that it is all right to ask for help (Cohn, 1982).

Other programs aim at specific activities. Because violent shaking of a baby can cause permanent brain injury or death and because many parents may not realize the danger of shaking, campaigns have been conducted to warn new parents about the dangers of this behavior. The "Don't Shake the Baby" program (Showers, 1992) was based on research showing that at least 25%, and possibly as much as 50%, of parents were unaware that shaking a baby is dangerous. The program aims at emphasizing to new parents that infant crying is normal and that shaking babies is dangerous. Cards are used to provide education on how to manage infant crying, focusing on safe alternatives to shaking the baby. The majority of parents who returned a questionnaire about the effectiveness of this advice given when their baby was born indicated that most found the information helpful. Forty-nine percent said that they would now be less likely to shake their baby.

Most of the interest in primary prevention programs aimed at children is in sexual abuse prevention. During the 1980s, there was a proliferation of such programs. Their aim is to teach children about sexual abuse—for example, by telling them that others are not allowed to touch the private parts of their bodies. Such programs teach children to refuse approaches by adults that might involve "bad touching," no matter who that person is. They tell the children that it is important to inform their parents or other adult if such an incident occurs, and they use a variety of techniques, which include films, slides, skits, lectures, puppets, stories, coloring books, and songs. The target age is usually young, grade school children. These programs became rapidly adopted throughout the school system. Relatively easy to implement, proponents believe that the programs have an impact on sexual abuse prevention. As a result, such programs became widely adopted without being carefully evaluated.

While it is easy to convey information to a child and then to test that child at a later date to see if this information is retained, the retention of such information may have little relationship to whether or not this knowledge leads to a change in behavior in a potentially abusive situation. Concerns have also been raised as to whether these programs make children unnecessarily anxious. There is also the problem that such programs may encourage complacency, with adults feeling that their duty to protect their children is met once their child has been exposed to a protective behaviors program. It is unreasonable to make a child entirely responsible for her own protection and unreasonable to expect that a child who has participated in a protective behaviors class will always be able to resist the charm and cunning of an experienced pedophile. Because child sexual abuse is so common, these programs often result in children telling their teacher that they have been abused. This is an important outcome for the program, but it is also important for schools using these programs to have in place procedures that allow such disclosures to be assessed with sensitivity and expertise.

It is difficult to demonstrate a change in behavior in children when they are in an abusive situation, but these programs have been shown to create a climate where children and their parents can discuss sexual abuse. Two-thirds of parents discussed sexual abuse with their children after such a program (Daro, Duerr, & Le Prohn, 1986) and 80% of parents reported that their children talked to them about the danger of sexual abuse following exposure to a protective behaviors program (Wurtele, 1988).

Demonstrating a change in behavior is much more difficult. "The ultimate goal of any program to prevent sexual abuse should be to teach behaviors so that when an adult makes a sexual advance toward a child, the child will react in an appropriate manner by saying 'No' and telling a responsible adult what happened" (Leventhal, 1987). Several studies have tried to determine whether a change in behavior actually occurs. The first two had very small samples. Peterson (1984) trained children to avoid strangers who tried to gain admittance at the door or who tried to determine by telephone if the child was at home alone. Three children were taught this, using behavioral techniques that included role play and rewards for desired behavior. Three other children participated in discussion groups on the subject. On posttesting, the children who had behavioral training had higher scores. Each child was then exposed to an investigator posing as a repairman who called at the child's own home and who telephoned them. Again, the children who had been taught using behavioral techniques were more likely to refuse to admit the stranger or to resist giving information on the telephone. However, when a stranger was encountered outside the home, appropriate safe responses were no different in either group, suggesting that training may have little value in being able to be generalized to other potentially dangerous situations.

In a similar study, this time with only three subjects in total, preschool children were trained to avoid strangers in the preschool playground (Poche, Brouwer, & Swearingen, 1981). They were taught to go to their teacher and ask permission if an adult asked them to leave the school playground. When the three children were approached individually by a stranger who asked them to leave the playground, each responded as he or she had been taught. These small studies suggest that it is possible to teach

young children behaviors that will be applied in a potentially dangerous situation, although it is less clear whether
they are able to generalize these principles to other situations. These studies also have some ethical problems about
whether children should be involved in this type of experi-
ment where there is the potential for them to become
frightened.

One study that did address this problem used a larger
sample of children and also took care to ensure that the
children were carefully monitored after the study for any
side effects such as anxiety (Fryer et al., 1987). Forty-four
kindergarten children were randomly allocated to a control group and a training group that received a 20-minute
session of child abuse prevention instruction for eight
days. They were taught that when alone in the presence of
a strange adult they should stay an arm's length away, not
talk or answer any questions, not take anything from the
stranger, and not go anywhere with the stranger.

A person brought in to play the role of the stranger then
approached the children individually on the school grounds
and asked each child to come to his car to help carry some
things for his son's birthday party or else to come to the car
to help carry some puppets into the school for a puppet
show that day. Forty-eight percent of the children in the
control group were prepared to go with the stranger compared with 22% of the group that had received child abuse
prevention training. More important perhaps, those children in the group that had received training and who
resisted going with the stranger had higher self-esteem
scores than their peers who agreed to go with the stranger.
This suggests that good self-esteem by itself may be a
protective factor.

Now that preventive programs have been widely used
for several years, there is the opportunity to retrospectively
ask the participants about the value of these programs in
subsequent real-life situations. When a representative
sample of 2000 children from the United States and their
caretakers were interviewed about their experiences with

child abuse and victimization programs (Finkelhor & Dziuba-Leatherman, 1995; Finkelhor, Asdigian, & Dziuba-Leatherman, 1995), it was found that two-thirds of the children had been exposed to at least one program at some time and 37% had been exposed within the past year. When children were asked to recall concrete situations in which the program information had been useful to them, 40% said it had specifically helped them to get out of fights and to avoid suspicious strangers. A quarter said that they had used the information to help a friend, 14% remembered a time when they decided to tell an adult about something because of what they had learned in the program and 5% said there had been some time when they had said "No" to an adult and had thought of the program.

However, the programs also seemed to produce anxiety in some children. Ten percent of the children said that they were fearful of adults as a result of the program and 15% of parents said that the program had made their child more anxious in general. These fears more were common among children who were younger, black and of lower socioeconomic status, presumably a more vulnerable group. Yet, these children and their parents also reported the most positive feelings about the program, which may indicate that the level of anxiety was based in reality for some of these children.

This type of evidence suggests that these programs can, in some instances, help children to protect themselves when in dangerous situations. A fringe benefit is that the programs do give children an opportunity to disclose prior abuse or current abuse (Daro, 1991). This disclosure enables action to be taken to protect the child who is currently being abused and may enable treatment to be provided to help other children deal with the emotional trauma of previous abuse. This, of course, presupposes that schools that use these programs are prepared to deal appropriately with disclosures.

The important thing to remember is that school prevention programs, while now appearing to be valuable in

helping some children to behave appropriately in dangerous situations, are just part of the package of child abuse
prevention. Cohn (1986) has listed a number of suggestions that could form an overall rationale for designing
prevention strategies. These include:

1. Child abuse is a very complex problem requiring
   multiple prevention strategies.

2. Knowledge about child abuse and its prevention is imperfect, suggesting that any preventive
   strategies cannot be based entirely on empirical
   findings.

3. There is no profile of a typical child abuser. This
   means that preventive efforts cannot be restricted
   to individuals who are thought to be high-risk
   abusers. This applies to sexual abusers as well as
   to physical abusers.

4. Because behaviors that lead to sexual abuse can
   begin before adulthood, preventive efforts should
   also be directed toward adolescents.

5. Sexual abuse is not strictly an issue of power, but
   involves sexual ideas, beliefs, misconceptions,
   and preferences. Prevention efforts should address these issues. These principles also apply to
   physical abuse.

6. Sexual abuse exists in part because of the values
   and messages that are transmitted to everyone
   through the media. Strongly voiced views, such as
   saying that it is not okay to molest children, should
   be promulgated.

7. Sexual abuse exists partly because children do not
   know how to resist abuse.

8. Physical and sexual abuse exists in part because
   children are sometimes in environments where
   they do not receive adequate protection.

9. Child abuse is a problem that is so deeply embed-

ded in societal values that there is no single law and no single professional able to handle the problem alone.

10. Public understanding of the problem of child abuse and public support for prevention programs are essential.

Given these assumptions, a comprehensive approach to prevention (Cohn, 1990) would include:

1. *Education for adolescents and younger children.* This involves providing all adolescents with quality sex education, including healthy sexuality, during their preteen and teenage years to enhance knowledge of what is normal and abnormal and to teach how to ask for help.

2. *Training for professionals and volunteers who work with children.* This involves teaching these individuals how to identify and help children who are being abused, how to teach children to protect themselves from abuse, and how to screen those who work with children who may be potential abusers.

3. *Preventive education for children.* This includes providing all school-age (and perhaps preschool) children with quality, ongoing education about how to protect themselves from abuse and what to do should it happen.

4. *Education for parents.* Providing all new parents with quality education and support to enhance early attachment and bonding at the time their baby is born. This should include information about appropriate and inappropriate touching, how to detect in oneself and one's mate an inclination toward inappropriate touch. How to cope with anger and stress associated with child-rearing and how to enhance the development of self-esteem in each other and in their children.

5. *Ensuring that all institutions involved with children, such as schools, youth groups, and after-school programs, train children in self-awareness and self-protection.* This involves having guidelines and regulations in place to screen, train, and monitor volunteers and staff.

6. *Public education that creates an environment in which the above preventive programs and concepts are effectively communicated.* Two different sets of messages are important. Adults and adolescents need messages that say:

> "Child abuse is a crime."
>
> "There is help available."
>
> "Abuse is a chronic problem unless you get help."
>
> "Children's emotions as well as their bodies are injured when they are physically or sexually abused."
>
> "Children cannot consent to this type of behavior."

The second set of messages is for children and should include:

> "It's okay to say, No."
>
> "It's not your fault."
>
> "Ask for help if this starts to happen to you."
>
> "Help is available."

7. *Treatment for the perpetrator.* Abusers need therapeutic assistance to increase the likelihood that they will stop abusing or molesting children. This will reduce the number of victims.

While listing the strategies is simpler than actually putting them into place, having them available is a start for beginning more prevention programs.

The problem of child abuse is a large one, the size of which has been recognized in recent years only as community and professional awareness has increased. It is likely that there will never be enough professional resources to cope effectively with all of the recognized cases, so that measures have to be taken at two levels. The first, the theme of this chapter, is the prevention of child abuse. This has to involve a change in community attitudes so that society is able to talk openly about the problem and take a firm stand that abuse of children in all its forms is unacceptable. This requires community education, preventative programs to teach children how to avoid sexual abuse inside and outside the family, programs to help parents of young children to cope with some of the stresses of child-rearing, and widespread availability of appropriate community resources. It also involves a caring society that provides opportunities for parents in circumstances of stress and poverty to receive assistance in their child-rearing.

The second level is to ensure that child abuse cases are managed effectively. This requires cooperation and education for the various professions likely to be involved in these cases. When courts become involved in these cases, it is important that the cases be dealt with expeditiously and in such a way that they do not cause further stress on the child and family. There must be a sentencing structure that emphasizes rehabilitation so that the needs of the child and family can be balanced with the needs of society to see that there are appropriate sanctions against those who abuse children. It is necessary to further the development of skills and understanding with regard to the problem, including the psychological assessment of the child and family, the physical assessment of the child, and the legal aspects of abuse, including how to be an advocate for the abused child in court, and the provision of ongoing, often long-term management.

Although child abuse may never be eliminated, we do know enough about prevention to be able to reduce its incidence if there is a public, political, and professional will to do so. We also understand enough about treatment to ensure that for those cases where prevention has not been possible, treatment can be provided at a level of quality that will have long-lasting beneficial effect. This will require a professional commitment to excellence based on good research and a public and political commitment to recognizing its value.

RESOURCES

Child Abuse and Neglect: The International Journal
    Editorial Office:
    1205 Oneida Street
    Denver, Colorado 80220
    (Child Abuse and Neglect is the journal of the
    International Society for the Prevention of Child
    Abuse and Neglect.)

Child Abuse Review
    Editorial Office:
    Newcomen Center, Guy's Hospital
    St. Thomas Street
    London SE1 9RT
    England

Child Maltreatment
    Editorial Office:
    407 S. Dearborn, Suite 1300
    Chicago, Illinois 60605

Journal of Child Sexual Abuse
    Editorial Office:
    The Hawthorn Press
    10 Alice Street
    Binghamton, New York 13904

Journal of Interpersonal Violence
    Editorial Office:
    Sage Publications
    2455 Teller Road
    Thousand Oaks, California 91320

Violence Update
    Editorial Office:
    School of Social Service Administration
    University of Chicago
    966 East 60th Street
    Chicago, Illinois 60637

BOOKS

A. Bentovim, E. Elton, J. Hildebrand, M. Tranter, &
E. Vizard (Eds.). *Child Sexual Abuse Within the
Family: Assessment and Treatment.* London:
Wright, 1987.

D. C. Bross & L. F. Michaels (Eds.). *Foundations of
Child Advocacy: Legal Representation for the
Maltreated Child.* Longmont, CO: Bookmakers
Guild, 1987.

L. De Mause (Ed.). *The History of Childhood.*
London: Bellew Publishing, 1991.

D. Finkelhor (Ed.). *A Sourcebook on Child Sexual
Abuse.* Newbury Park, CA: Sage Publications,
1986.

D. Finkelhor & L. M. Williams. *Nursery Crimes: Sexual Abuse in Day Care.* Newbury Park, CA: Sage Publications, 1988.

W. N. Friedrich. *Casebook of Sexual Abuse Treatment.* New York: W. W. Norton, 1991.

T. Furniss. *The Multi-Professional Handbook of Child Sexual Abuse.* London: Rutledge, 1991.

J. Garbarino, E. Guttman, & J. Seeley. *The Psychologically Battered Child.* San Francisco: Jossey-Bass, 1986.

S. J. Emans & A. Heger. *Evaluation of the Sexually Abused Child: A Medical Textbook and Photographic Atlas.* New York: Oxford University Press, 1992.

R. S. Kempe, M. E. Helfer, & R. D. Klugman (Eds.). *The Battered Child* (5th ed.). Chicago: University of Chicago Press, 1996.

P. K. Kleinman. *Diagnostic Imaging of Child Abuse.* Williams and Wilkins, Baltimore, 1987.

S. Ludwig & A. Kornberg. *Child Abuse: A Medical Reference* (2nd ed.). New York: Churchill Livingstone, 1992.

K. MacFarlane & J. Waterman. *Sexual Abuse of Young Children.* New York: Guilford Press, 1986.

P. B. Mrazek & C. H. Kempe (Eds.). *Sexually Abused Children and Their Families.* New York: Pergamon Press, 1982.

R. K. Oates (Ed.). *Child Abuse and Neglect: What Happens Eventually?* New York: Brunner/Mazel, 1985.

R. K. Oates (Ed.). *Understanding and Managing Child Sexual Abuse.* Philadelphia: W. B. Saunders, 1990.

R. M. Reece (Ed.). *Child Abuse, Medical Diagnosis and Management.* Malvern, PA: Lea and Febiger, 1994.

G. D. Ryan & S. L. Lane. *Juvenile Sexual Offending: Causes, Consequences and Correction.* Lexington, MA: Lexington Books, 1991.

S. M. Sgroi. *Handbook of Clinical Intervention in Child Sexual Abuse.* Lexington, MA: Lexington Books, 1982.

D. J. Willis, E. W. Holden, & M. Rosenberg. *Prevention of Child Maltreatment: Development and Ecological Perspectives.* New York: Wiley, 1992.

K. Wurtele & C. L. Miller-Perrin. *Preventing Child Abuse.* Lincoln: University of Nebraska Press, 1992.

G. Wyatt & G. Powell. *Lasting Effects of Child Sexual Abuse.* Newbury Park, CA: Sage Publications, 1988.

ORGANIZATIONS

United States

American Humane Association
American Association for Protecting Children
9725 East Hampden Avenue
Denver, Colorado 80231

American Professional Society on the Abuse of
  Children
407 South Dearborn, Suite 1300
Chicago, Illinois 60605

C. Henry Kempe National Center for the Prevention
  and Treatment of Child Abuse and Neglect
1205 Oneida Street
Denver, Colorado 80220

National Center for the Prosecution of Child Abuse
1033 North Fairfax, Suite 200
Alexandria, Virginia 22314

National Clearing House on Child Abuse and
  Neglect
P.O. Box 1182
Washington, DC 20013

National Committee to Prevent Child Abuse
332 South Michigan Avenue, Suite 1600
Chicago, Illinois 60604

International

The International Society for the Prevention of
  Child Abuse and Neglect
332 South Michigan Avenue, Suite 1600
Chicago, Illinois 60604

Australia

National Association for the Prevention of Child
  Abuse and Neglect
GPO Box 3658
Sydney 2001

National Child Protection Clearing House
Australian Institute of Family Studies
300 Queen Street
Melbourne, Victoria 3000

New Zealand

Child Protection Trust
Building 43, Auckland Hospital
Private Bag 92024
Auckland

United Kingdom

The National Society for the Prevention of Cruelty
    to Children
67 Saffron Hill
London EC1N 8RS

REFERENCES

Abel, G., Rouleau, J., & Cunningham-Rathner, J. (1986). Sexually aggressive behaviour. In W. Curran, A. McGarry, & S. Skoh (Eds.), *Psychiatry and psychology: Perspectives and standards for intradisciplinary practice*. Philadelphia: Davis.

Adams-Tucker, C. (1982). Proximate effects of sexual abuse in childhood: A report on 28 children. *American Journal of Psychiatry, 139,* 1252–1256.

Allen, A., & Morton, A. (1961). *This is your child*. London: Routledge & Kegan Paul

American Academy of Pediatrics, Committee on School Health. (1991). Corporal punishment in schools. *Pediatrics, 88,* 173.

Ammerman, R., Van Hasselt, V., Hersen, M., McConigle, J., & Lubetsky, M. (1989). Abuse and neglect in psychiatrically hospitalized multi-handicapped children. *Child Abuse and Neglect, 13,* 335–343.

Angus, A., & Wilkinson, K. (1993). *Child abuse and neglect in Australia, 1990–1991*. (Australian Institute of Health and Welfare. Child Welfare, Series no. 2). Canberra: Australia Government Printing Service.

Araji, S., & Finkelhor, D. (1986). Abusers: A review of the research. In D. Finkelhor (Ed.), *A sourcebook on child sexual abuse*. Newbury Park CA: Sage.

Astley, R. (1953). Multiple metaphyseal fractures in small children (metaphyseal fragility of bone). *British Journal of Radiology, 26,* 577–583.

Bagley, C., & Ramsay, R. (1986). Sexual abuse in childhood: Psychosocial outcomes and implications for social work practice. *Journal of Social Work and Human Sexuality, 4,* 33–47.

Bakan, D. (1971). *Slaughter of the innocents: A study of the battered child phenomenon.* San Francisco: Jossey-Bass.

Bakwin, H. (1949). Emotional deprivation in infants. *Journal of Pediatrics, 35,* 512–521.

Bays, J. (1990). Substance abuse and child abuse. *Pediatric Clinics of North America, 37,* 881–904.

Bays, J., & Chadwick, D. (1993). Medical diagnosis of the sexually abused child. *Child Abuse and Neglect, 17,* 91–110.

Belsky, J., & Vondra, J. (1989). Lessons from child abuse: The determinants of parenting. In D. Cicchetti & V. Carlson (Eds.), *Child maltreatment: Research and theory on the consequences of abuse and neglect* (pp. 153–202). New York: Cambridge University Press.

Beraud, J. B. (1839). *Les filles publiques de Paris.* Paris.

Black, R., & Mayer, J. (1980). Parents with special problems: Alcoholism and opiate addiction. *Child Abuse and Neglect, 4,* 45–54.

Bools, C., Neale, B., & Meadow, R. (1994). Munchausen syndrome by proxy: A study of psychopathology. *Child Abuse and Neglect, 18,* 773–778.

Booth, S. M. (1990). Interviewing the parents. In R. K. Oates (Ed.), *Understanding and managing child sexual abuse.* Philadelphia: W. B. Saunders.

Bowlby, J. (1951). *Maternal care and mental health.* Geneva: World Health Organization.

Bowlby, J. (1969). *Attachment and loss. Vol 1: Attachment.* New York: Basic Books.

Brazelton, T. B. (1982). Joint regulation of neonate-parent behaviour. In E. Z. Tronick (Ed.), *Social interchange in infancy: Affect, cognition and communication.* Baltimore: University Park Press.

Briere, J. (1984). *The effects of childhood sexual abuse on later psychological functioning: Defining a 'post-sexual abuse syndrome'.* Paper presented at the third National Conference on Sexual Victimization of Children, Washington, DC.

Briere, J., & Runtz, M. (1988). Symptomatology associated with childhood sexual victimization in a non-clinical adult sample. *Child Abuse and Neglect, 12,* 51–59.

Brown, S. E. (1984). Social class, child maltreatment and delinquent behaviour. *Criminology, 22,* 259–278.

Browne, A., & Finkelhor, D. (1986). Initial and long-term effects: A review of the research. In D. Finkelhor (Ed.), *A sourcebook on child sexual abuse.* Newbury Park, CA: Sage.

Burgdorff, K. (1980). *Recognition and reporting of child maltreatment: Findings from the national study of the incidence and severity of child abuse and neglect.* Washington, DC: National Center on Child Abuse and Neglect.

Burns, N., Williams, L., & Finkelhor, D. (1988). Victim Impact. In D. Finkelhor & L. Williams (Eds.), *Nursery crimes: Sexual abuse in day care.* Newbury Park, CA: Sage.

Burton, L. (1968). *Vulnerable children.* London: Routledge and Kegan Paul.

Caffey, J. (1946). Multiple fractures in the long bones of infants suffering from chronic subdural hematoma. *American Journal of Roentgenology, 56,* 163–173.

Chapin, H.D. (1915a). A plea for accurate statistics in infants' institutions. *Archives of Pediatrics, 32,* 724–726.

Chapin, H.D. (1915b). Are institutions for infants necessary? *Journal of the American Medical Association,
64*, 1–3.

Cohn, A. (1982). The role of media campaigns in preventing child abuse. In R. K. Oates (Ed.), *Child
abuse: A community concern.* New York: Brunner/
Mazel.

Cohn, A. H. (1986). Preventing adults from becoming
sexual molesters. *Child Abuse and Neglect, 10,*
559–562.

Cohn, A. H. (1990). Education as a means of prevention.
In R. K. Oates (Ed.), *Understanding and managing
child sexual abuse.* Philadelphia: W. B. Saunders.

Cohn, A., & Daro, D. (1987). Is treatment too late: What
ten years of evaluative research tells us. *Child Abuse
and Neglect, 11,* 433–442.

Coleman, R. W., & Provence, S. (1957). Environmental
retardation (hospitalism) in infants living in families.
Pediatrics, 19, 285–292.

Collings, S. (1995). The long-term effects of contact and
non-contact forms of child sexual abuse in a sample
of university men. *Child Abuse and Neglect, 19,*
1–6.

Colorado Child Fatality Review Committee. (1990).
Preventing child death: A challenge for the 90's.
Denver: Colorado Department of Social Services.

Corwin, D. (1988). Early diagnosis of child sexual abuse:
Diminishing the lasting effects. In G. Wyatt & G.
Powell (Eds.), *Lasting effects of child sexual abuse.*
Newbury Park, CA: Sage.

Creighton, S. J., & Noyes, P. (1989). *Child abuse trends
in England and Wales 1983–87.* London: National
Society for Prevention of Cruelty to Children.

Culpe, R. E., Heide, J. S., & Richardson, M. T. (1987).
Maltreated children's developmental scores: Treatment versus non-treatment. *Child Abuse and Neglect, 11,* 29–34.

Daro, D. (1991). Child sexual abuse and prevention:

Separating fact from fiction. *Child Abuse and Neglect, 15,* 1–4.

Daro, D., Duerr, J., & Le Prohn, N. (1986). *Child assault prevention instruction: What works with preschoolers.* Chicago: National Committee for the Prevention of Child Abuse and Neglect.

Daro, D., & McCurdy, K. (1993). *Current trends in child abuse reporting and fatalities: The results of the 1993 Annual Fifty State Survey.* Chicago: National Committee for the Prevention of Child Abuse and Neglect.

De Francis, V. (1969). *Protecting the child victim of sex crimes committed by adults.* Denver: American Humane Association.

De Mause, L. (1974). The evolution of childhood. In L. De Mause (Ed.), *The History of Childhood.* New York: Psychohistory Press.

DeSilva, S., & Oates, R. K. (1993). Child homicide: The extreme of child abuse. *Medical Journal of Australia, 158,* 300–301.

Durfee, M. (1989). Fatal child abuse: Intervention and prevention. *Protecting Children. Spring,* 9–12.

Emans, S. J. (1992). Physical evaluation of the child and adolescent. In S. J. Emans & A. Heger (Eds.), *Evaluation of the sexually abused child: A medical textbook and photographic atlas.* New York: Oxford University Press.

Emans, S. J., & Heger, A. (Eds.). (1992). *Evaluation of the sexually abused child: A medical textbook and photographic atlas.* New York: Oxford University Press.

Eckenrode, J., Laird, M., & Doris, J. (1995). School performance and disciplinary problems among abused and neglected children. *Developmental Psychology, 29,* 53–62.

Egeland, B., Stroufe, A., & Erickson, M. (1983). The developmental consequence of different patterns of maltreatment. *Child Abuse and Neglect, 7,* 459–469.

Elmer, E., & Gregg, G. (1967). Developmental characteristics of abused children. *Pediatrics, 40*, 569–602.

Elmer, E., Gregg, G., & Ellison, P. (1969). Late results of
the failure to thrive syndrome. *Clinical Pediatrics, 8*,
584–588.

English, P. C. (1978). Failure to thrive without organic
reason. *Pediatric Annals, 7*, 774–781.

Everson, M. D., & Boat, B. W. (1994). Putting the anatomical doll controversy in perspective. *Child Abuse
and Neglect, 18*, 113–129.

Feldman, K. W. (1993). When is childhood drowning
neglect? *Child Abuse and Neglect, 17*, 329–336.

Finkelhor, D. (1984). *Child sexual abuse: New theory
and research.* New York: Free Press.

Finkelhor, D. (1986). Abusers: Special topics. In D.
Finkelhor (Ed.), *A sourcebook on child sexual
abuse.* Newbury Park, CA : Sage.

Finkelhor, D., Asdigian, N., & Dziuba-Leatherman, J.
(1995). The effectiveness of victimization prevention
instruction: An evaluation of children's responses to
actual threats and assaults. *Child Abuse and Neglect, 19*, 141–153.

Finkelhor, D., & Baron, L. (1986). High-risk children. In
D. Finkelhor (Ed.), *A sourcebook on child sexual
abuse.* Newbuy Park, CA: Sage.

Finkelhor, D., & Dziuba-Leatherman, J. (1995). Victimization prevention programs: A national survey of
children's responses and reactions. *Child Abuse and
Neglect, 19*, 129–139.

Finkelhor, D., & Russell, D. E. H. (1984). Women as
perpetrators. In D. Finkelhor (Ed.), *Child sexual
abuse.* New York: Free Press.

Finkelhor, D., & Williams, L. (1988a). Introduction,
study design and incidence. In D. Finkelhor & L.
Williams (Eds.), *Nursery crimes: Sexual abuse in
day care.* Newbury Park, CA: Sage.

Finkelhor, D., & Williams, L. (1988b). Summary and

recommendations for parents and professionals. In D. Finkelhor & L. Williams (Eds.), *Nursery crimes: Sexual abuse in day care.* Newbury Park, CA: Sage.

Finkelhor, D., & Williams, L. (1988c). *Nursery crimes: Sexual abuse in day care.* Newbury Park, CA: Sage.

Fraser, B. G. (1976). The child and his parents: A delicate balance of rights. In R. E. Helfer & C. H. Kempe (Eds.), *Child abuse and neglect: The family and the community.* Cambridge, MA: Ballinger.

Fraser, B. G. (1981). Sexual child abuse: The legislation and the law in the United States. In P. B. Mrazek & C. H. Kempe (Eds.), *Sexually abused children and their families.* Oxford: Pergamon.

Freud, S. (1986). The aetiology of hysteria. In J. Strachey (Ed. and Trans.), *The standard edition of the complete psychological works of Sigmund Freud, Vol. 3.* London: Hogarth Press.

Friedrich, W., Beilke, R., & Urquiza, A. (1988). Behaviour problems in young sexually abused boys. *Journal of Interpersonal Violence, 3,* 21–28.

Friedrich, W. N., Urquiza, A. J., & Beilke, R. L. (1986). Behaviour problems in sexually abused young children. *Journal of Pediatric Psychology, 11,* 45–57.

Frude, N., & Goss, A. (1980). Maternal anger and the young child. In N. Frude (Ed.), *Psychological approaches to child abuse.* London: Batsford Academic Press.

Fryer, G. E., Kraizer, S., & Miyoshi, T. (1987). Measuring actual reduction of risk to child abuse: A new approach. *Child Abuse and Neglect, 11,* 173–179.

Fryer, G. E., & Miyoshi, T. J. (1994). A survival analysis of the revictimization of children: The case of Colorado. *Child Abuse and Neglect, 18,* 1063–1071.

Furniss, T. (1990). Common mistakes and how to avoid them. In R. K. Oates (Ed.), *Understanding and managing child sexual abuse.* Philadelphia: W. B. Saunders.

Gaensbauer, T., & Sands, K. (1970). Distorted effective
    communication in abused/neglected infants and
    their potential impact on caretakers. *Journal of the
    American Academy of Child Psychiatry, 18,*
    236–249.
Gagnon, J. (1965). Female child victims of sexual of-
    fences. *Social Problems, 13,* 176–192.
Galler, J. R., Ramsey, F., & Forde, V. (1985). A follow-up
    study of the influence of early malnutrition on
    subsequent development. *Nutrition and Behavior, 3,*
    211–222.
Garbarino, J. (1989). The psychologically battered child:
    Towards a definition. *Pediatric Annals, 18,*
    502–504.
Garbarino, J., Guttman, E., & Seeley, J. W. (1986). *The
    psychologically battered child.* San Francisco:
    Jossey-Bass.
Gelles, R. J. (1978). Violence towards children in the
    United States. *American Journal of Orthopsychiatry,
    48,* 580–592.
Gelles, R. J., & Cornell, C. P. (1990). *Intimate violence in
    families.* (2nd ed.), London: Sage.
George, C., & Maine, M. (1979). Social interactions of
    young, abused children: Approach, avoidance and
    aggression. *Child Development, 50,* 306–318.
Goodman, G., Taub, E., Jones, D., England, P., Port, L.,
    Rudy, L., & Prado, L. (1992) Testifying in criminal
    court: emotional effects on child sexual assault
    victims. *Monographs of the Society for Research in
    Child Development, 57,* 5.
Graham, H. (1980). Mothers' accounts of anger and
    aggression towards their babies. In N. Frude (Ed.),
    Psychological approaches to child abuse. London:
    Batsford Academic Press.
Gray, J. D., Cutler, C. A., Dean, J. G., & Kempe, C. H.
    (1977). Prediction and prevention of child abuse
    and neglect. *Child Abuse and Neglect, 1,* 45–58.
Green, A. H. (1978). Psychopathology of abused chil-

dren. *Journal of the American Academy of Child Psychiatry, 17,* 92–103.

Groothuis, J., Altemeier, W., Robarge, J., O'Connor, S., Sandler, H., Vietze, P., & Lustig, J. (1982). Increased child abuse in families with twins. *Pediatrics, 70,* 769–773.

Haynes, C. F., Cutler, C., Gray, J., & Kempe, R. S. (1984). Hospitalized cases of non-organic failure to thrive: The scope of the problem and short-term lay health visitor intervention. *Child Abuse and Neglect, 8,* 229–242.

Heckler, S. (1994). Letter to the Editor. *Child Abuse and Neglect, 18,* 539–540.

Herrenkohl, E., & Herrenkohl, R. (1979). A comparison of abused children and their siblings. *Journal of the American Academy of Child Psychiatry, 18,* 260–269.

Herrenkohl, R. C., Herrenkohl, E. C., & Egolf, B. P. (1981). Some antecedents and developmental consequences of child maltreatment. In R. Rizley & D. Cicchetti (Eds.), *Developmental perspectives on child maltreatment.* San Francisco: Jossey Bass.

Hobbs, C. J. (1984). Skull fracture and the diagnosis of child abuse. *Archives of Disease of Childhood, 39,* 246–252.

Hobbs, C. J. (1993). Fractures. In R. Meadows (Ed.), *ABC of child abuse.* London: BMJ.

Hobbs, C. J., Hanks, H. G., & Wynne, J. M. (1993). Clinical aspects of sexual abuse. In *Child abuse and neglect: A clinician's handbook.* London: Churchill Livingstone.

Illick, J. E. (1974). Anglo-American child rearing. In L. De Mause (Ed.), *The history of childhood.* New York: Psychohistory Press.

Jacobson, R., & Straker, G. (1982). Peer group interaction of physically abused children. *Child Abuse and Neglect, 6,* 321–327.

Jeffcoate, J. A., Humphrey, M. E., & Lloyd, J. K. (1979).

Disturbance in parent–child relationship following
pre-term delivery. *Developmental Medicine and
Child Neurology, 21*, 344–352.

Jones, D. P. H. (1987). The untreatable family. *Child
Abuse and Neglect, 11*, 409–420.

Jones, D. P. H. (1990). Talking with children. In R. K.
Oates (Ed.), *Understanding and managing child
sexual abuse.* Philadelphia: W. B. Saunders.

Jones, D. P. H. (1991). Ritualism and child sexual abuse.
Child Abuse and Neglect, 15, 163–170.

Jones, D. P. H. (1994). Autism, facilitated communication and allegations of child abuse and neglect.
Child Abuse and Neglect, 18, 491–493.

Kaplan, S. J., Pelcovitz, D., Salzinger, S., & Ganeles, D.
(1983). Psychopathology of parents of abused and
neglected children and adolescents. *Journal of the
American Academy of Child Psychiatry, 22*,
238–244.

Kaufman, J., & Zigler, E. (1987). Do abused children
become abusive parents? *American Journal of
Orthopsychiatry, 57*, 186.

Kelley, S. J., Brant, R., & Waterman, J. (1993). Sexual
abuse of children in day care centers. *Child Abuse
and Neglect, 17*, 71–89.

Kempe, C. H. (1978). Sexual abuse, another hidden
problem. *Pediatrics, 62*, 382–389.

Kempe, C. H., & Helfer, R. E. (1972). *Helping the battered child and his family.* Philadelphia: J. B.
Lippincott.

Kempe, C. H., Silverman, F. N., Steele, B. F.,
Droegmueller, W., & Silver, H. K. (1962). The bat-
tered child syndrome. *Journal of the American
Medical Association, 181*, 17–24.

Kempe, R. S., Cutler, C., & Dean, J. (1980). The infant
with failure to thrive. In C. H. Kempe & R. E. Helfer
(Eds.), *The battered child* (3rd ed.) (pp. 163–182).
Chicago: University of Chicago Press.

Kinsey, A., Pomeroy, W., Martin, C, & Gebhard, P. (1953). *Sexual behavior in the human female.* Philadelphia: W. B. Saunders.

Korbin, J. (1977). Anthropological contributions to the study of child abuse. *Child Abuse and Neglect, 1,* 7–24.

Korbin, J. (1980). The cross-cultural context of child abuse and neglect. In C. H. Kempe & R. E. Helfer (Eds.), *The battered child* (3rd ed.). Chicago: University of Chicago Press.

Kovacs, G., Matthiesson, H., Westcott, M., Dunn, K., & Bennison, M. (1984). Postcoital intervention. *Medical Journal of Australia, 141,* 425–426.

Ladson, S., Johnson, C. F., & Doty, R. E. (1987). Do physicians recognize sexual abuse? *American Journal of Diseases of Children, 141,* 411–415.

Lally, R. (1984). Three views of child neglect: Expanding visions of preventive intervention. *Child Abuse and Neglect, 8,* 243–254.

Lamb, M. E. (1994). The investigation of child sexual abuse: An interdisciplinary consensus statement. *Child Abuse and Neglect, 18,* 1021–1028.

Lazoritz, S. (1990). Whatever happened to Mary Ellen? *Child Abuse and Neglect, 14,* 143–149.

Leventhal, J. (1987). Programs to prevent sexual abuse: What outcomes should be measured? *Child Abuse and Neglect, 11,* 169–172.

Leventhal, J. (1990). Epidemiology of child sexual abuse. In R. K. Oates (Ed.), *Understanding and managing child sexual abuse.* Philadelphia: W. B. Saunders.

Lusk, R., & Waterman, J. (1986). Effects of sexual abuse on children. In K. MacFarlane & J. Waterman (Eds.), *Sexual abuse of young children.* New York: Guildford Press.

Lynch, M. A. (1976). Risk factors in the child: A study of abused children and their siblings. In H. P. Martin (Ed.), *The abused child.* Cambridge, MA: Ballinger.

Lynch, M. A., & Roberts, J. (1977). Predicting child abuse: Signs of bonding failure in the maternity hospital. *British Medical Journal, 1*, 624–626.

Lynch, M. A., & Roberts, J. (1982). *Consequences of child abuse.* London: Academic Press.

Lyons, T. J., & Oates, R. K. (1993). Falling out of bed: A relatively benign occurrence. *Pediatrics, 92*, 125–127.

Mannarino, A. P., & Cohen, J. A. (1986). A clinical-demographic study of sexually abused children. *Child Abuse and Neglect, 10*, 17–23.

Martin, H. P. (1972). The child and his development. In C. H. Kempe & R. E. Helfer (Eds.), *Helping the battered child and his family.* Philadelphia: Lippincott.

Martin, H. P., & Beezley, P. (1977). Behavioural observations on abused children. *Developmental Medicine and Child Neurology, 19*, 373–378.

Martin, J., & Elmer, E. (1992). Battered children grown up: A follow-up study of individuals severely maltreated as children. *Child Abuse and Neglect, 16*, 75–87.

Masson, J. (1984). *Freud: The assault on truth: Freud's suppression of seduction theory.* London: Faber and Faber.

Matthews, C. (1990). *Breaking through.* London: Lion Press.

McRae, K. N., & Longstaffe, S. E. (1982). The behaviour of battered children: An aid to diagnosis and management. In R. K. Oates (Ed.), *Child abuse: A community concern.* Sydney: Butterworths.

Meadow, R. (1977). Munchausen syndrome by proxy: The hinterland of child abuse. *Lancet, 2*, 343–345.

Morse, C. S., Sahler, O. J., & Friedman, S. B. (1970). A three-year follow-up of abused and neglected children. *American Journal of Diseases of Children, 120*, 439–446.

Mortiz, A. R., & Henriques, F. C. (1947). Studies of thermal injury II: The relative importance of time and surface temperature in the causation of cutaneous burns. *American Journal of Pathology, 23,* 695–720.

Mullen, R. E., Romans-Clarkson, S. E., Walton, V. A., & Herbison, G. P. (1988). Impact of sexual and physical abuse on women's mental health. *Lancet, 1,* 842–845.

Ney, P., Fung, T., & Wickett, A. (1994). The worst combination of child abuse and neglect. *Child Abuse and Neglect, 18,* 705–714.

Oates, R. K. (1984). Non-organic failure to thrive. *Australian Paediatric Journal, 20,* 95–100.

Oates, R. K. (1985). *Child abuse and neglect: What happens eventually?* New York: Brunner /Mazel.

Oates, R. K. (1993). Three do's and three don'ts for expert witnesses. *Child Abuse and Neglect, 17,* 571–572.

Oates, R. K., & Bross, D. L. (1995). What have we learned about treating child physical abuse: A literature review of the last decade. *Child Abuse and Neglect, 119*(4), 463–473.

Oates, R. K., Gray, J., Schweitzer, L., Kempe, R. S., & Harmon, R. J. (1995). A therapeutic preschool for abused children: The keepsafe project. *Child Abuse and Neglect, 19,* 1379–1386.

Oates, R. K., & Kempe, R. S. (1996). Growth failure in infants. In R. S. Kempe, M. E. Helfer, & R. D. Krugman (Eds.), *The battered child* (5th Ed.). Chicago: University of Chicago Press.

Oates, R. K., Lynch, D. I., Stern, A. E., O'Toole, B. I., & Cooney, G. (1995). The criminal justice system and the sexually abused child: help or hindrance? *Medical Journal of Australia, 162,* 126–130.

Oates, R. K., O'Toole, B. I., Lynch, D., Stern, A., & Cooney, G. (1994). Stability and change in outcomes for sexually abused children. *Journal of the American Academy of Child and Adolescent Psychiatry, 33*, 945–953.

Oates, R. K., Peacock, A., & Forrest, D. (1984). The development of abused children. *Developmental Medicine and Child Neurology, 26*, 649–656.

Oates, R. K., Peacock, A., & Forrest, D. (1985). Long-term effects of non-organic failure to thrive. *Pediatrics, 75*, 36–40.

Oates, R. K., & Tong, L. (1987). Sexual abuse of children: An area with room for professional reforms. *Medical Journal of Australia, 147*, 544–548.

Olds, D. L. (1993). *Home visitation 2000.* Denver: The Colorado Trust.

Olds, D. L., Henderson, C. R., Chamberlain, R., & Tatelbaum, R. (1986). Preventing child abuse and neglect: A randomized trial of nurse home visitation. *Pediatrics, 78*, 65–78.

Olds, D. L., Henderson, C. R., & Kitzman, H. (1994). Does prenatal and infancy home nurse visitation have enduring effects on qualities of parental care giving and child health at 25–50 months of life? *Pediatrics, 93*, 89–98.

Ounsted, C. V., & Lindsay, J. (1974). Aspects of bonding failure. *Developmental Medicine & Child Neurology, 16*, 447–456.

Paradise, J. (1989). Predictive accuracy and the diagnosis of sexual abuse: A big issue about a little tissue. *Child Abuse and Neglect, 13*, 169–176.

Patterson, G. R., & Thompson, M. (1980). Emotional child abuse and neglect: An exercise in definition. In R. Volpe, M. Breton, & J. Mitton (Eds.), *The maltreatment of the school-aged child.* Lexington, MA: Heath.

Perez, C., & Widom, C. S. (1994). Childhood victimization and long-term intellectual and academic outcomes. *Child Abuse and Neglect, 18*, 617–633.

Peters, S. D. (1988). Child sexual abuse and later psychological problems. In G. Wyatt & G. Powell (Eds.),

Lasting effects of child sexual abuse. Newbury Park, CA: Sage.

Peters, S., Wyatt, G., & Finkelhor, D. (1986). Prevalence. In D. Finkelhor (Ed.), *A sourcebook on child sexual abuse.* Newbury Park CA: Sage.

Peterson, L. (1984). Teaching home safety and survival skills to latch-key children. *Journal of Applied Behavior Analysis, 17,* 279–293.

Poche, C., Brouwer, R., & Swearingen, M. (1981). Teaching self-protection to young children. *Journal of Applied Behavior Analysis, 14,* 169–176.

Prino, C. T., & Peyrot, M. (1994). The effect of physical abuse and neglect on aggressive, withdrawn and prosocial behavior. *Child Abuse and Neglect, 18,* 871–884.

Radbill, S. X. (1974). A history of child abuse and infanticide. In R. E. Helfer & C. H. Kempe (Eds.), *The battered child* (2nd ed.). Chicago: University of Chicago Press.

Radbill, S. X. (1980). Children in a world of violence. In C. H. Kempe & R. E. Helfer (Eds.), *The battered child* (3rd ed.). Chicago: University of Chicago Press.

Reidy, T. (1977). The aggressive characteristics of abused and neglected children. *Journal of Clinical Psychology, 33,* 1140–1145.

Richardson, S. A. (1976). The relation of severe malnutrition in infancy to the intelligence of school children with differing life histories. *Pediatric Research, 10,* 57–61.

Rosenberg, D. (1987). Web of deceit: A literature review of Munchausen syndrome by proxy. *Child Abuse and Neglect, 11,* 547–563.

Runyan, D. K., Everson, M. D., Edelsohn, G. A., Hunter, W., & Coulter, M. (1988). Impact of legal intervention on sexually abused children. *Journal of Pediatrics, 113,* 647–653.

Russell, D. E. H. (1984). *Sexual exploitation.* Newbury Park, CA: Sage.

Rutter, M. (1967). A child's behaviour questionnaire for

completion by teachers. *Journal of Child Psychology and Psychiatry, 8*, 1–11.

Rutter, M. (1972). *Maternal deprivation reassessed.* Harmondsworth, Middlesex: Penguin.

Ryan, G. D., Metzner, J. L., & Krugman, R. D. (1990). When the abuser is a child. In R. K. Oates (Ed.), *Understanding and managing child sexual abuse.* Philadelphia: W. B. Saunders.

Schechter, M., & Roberge, L. (1976). Sexual exploitation. In R. E. Helfer, & C. H. Kempe (Eds.), *Child abuse and neglect: The family and the community.* Cambridge, MA: Ballinger.

Schmitt, B. D. (1981). Child Neglect. In N. S. Ellerstein (Ed.), *Child abuse and neglect: A medical reference.* New York: Wiley.

Schor, D. P. (1987). Sex and sexual abuse in developmentally disabled adolescents. *Seminars in Adolescent Medicine, 3*, 1–7.

Schwartz-Kenney, B. M., Wilson, M. E., & Goodman, G. S. (1990). An examination of child witness accuracy. In R. K. Oates (Ed.), *Understanding and managing child sexual abuse.* Philadelphia: W. B. Saunders.

Sedney, M. A., & Brooks, B. (1984). Factors associated with a history of childhood sexual experiences in a non-clinical female population. *Journal of the American Academy of Child Psychiatry, 23*, 215–218.

Sgroi, S., Blick, L., & Porter, F. (1982). A conceptual framework for child sexual abuse. In S. M. Sgroi (Ed.), *Handbook of clinical interventions in child sexual abuse.* Lexington, MA: Lexington Books.

Shaheen, E., Alexander, C., Truskowsky, M., & Barbero, G. J. (1968). Failure to thrive: A retrospective profile. *Clinical Pediatrics, 7*, 255–261.

Showers, J. (1992). "Don't Shake the Baby.": The effectiveness of a prevention program. *Child Abuse and Neglect, 16*, 11–18.

Silverman, F. N. (1953). The Roentgen manifestations of

unrecognized skeletal trauma in infants. *American Journal of Roentgenology, 69,* 413–427.

Skuse, D. W. (1989). Emotional abuse and neglect. *British Medical Journal, 298,* 1692–1694.

Solnit, A. J. (1984). Theoretical and practical aspects of risks and vulnerabilities in infancy. *Child Abuse and Neglect, 8,* 133–144.

Spitz, R. (1945). Hospitalism: An inquiry into the genesis of psychiatric conditions in early childhood. *Psychoanalytic Study of the Child, 1,* 53–74.

Steele, B. F. (1993). Personal communication.

Stern, A., Lynch, D., Oates, R. K., O'Toole, B. I., & Cooney, G. (1995). Self-esteem, depression, behaviour and family functioning in sexually abused children. *Journal of Child Psychology and Psychiatry 36,* 1077–1089.

Stevens, P., & Eide, M. (1990). The first chapter of children's rights. *American Heritage (July/August),* 84–91.

Stewart, D. (1992). Sexually transmitted diseases. In S. J. Emans & A. Heger (Eds.), *Evaluation of the sexually abused child: A medical textbook and photographic atlas.* New York: Oxford University Press.

Straus, M. A. (1980a). Stress and physical abuse. *Child Abuse and Neglect, 4,* 75–88.

Straus, M. A. (1980b). Social stress and marital violence in a national sample of American families. *Annals of the New York Academy of Science, 347,* 229–250.

Straus, M. A. (1991). Family violence in American families: Incidence notes, causes, and trends. In D. D. Knudsen & J. L. Miller (Eds.), *Abused and battered: Social and legal responses of family violence* (pp. 17–34). New York: Aldine de Gruyter.

Straus, M. A., Gelles, R. J., & Steinmetz, S. K. (1980). *Behind closed doors: Violence in the American family.* New York: Anchor Press.

Straus, M. A., & Kantor, G. K. (1987). Stress in child abuse. In C. H. Kempe & R. E. Helfer (Eds.), *The battered child* (4th ed.). Chicago: University of Chicago Press.

Summitt, R. C. (1983). The child sexual abuse accommodation syndrome. *Child Abuse and Neglect, 7,* 177–193.

Summitt, R. C. (1990). The specific vulnerability of children. In R. K. Oates (Ed.), *Understanding and managing child sexual abuse.* Philadelphia: W. B. Saunders.

Tardieu, A. (1860). Étude medico-legale sur les services et mauvais traitements exerces sur des enfants. In S. M. Smith (Ed.), *The battered child syndrome.* London: Butterworths.

Togut, M. R., Allen, J. E., & Lelchuck, L. (1969). A psychological exploration of the non–organic failure to thrive syndrome. *Developmental Medicine and Child Neurology, 11,* 601–607.

Tong, L., Oates, R. K., & McDowell, M. (1987). Personality development following child sexual abuse. *Child Abuse and Neglect, 11,* 371–383.

Tufts' New England Medical Center Division of Child Psychiatry. (1984). *Sexually exploited children: Service and research project.* US Department of Justice, Washington, D.C.

Van Meter, M. J. (1986). An alternative to foster care for victims of child abuse/neglect: A university-based program. *Child Abuse and Neglect, 10,* 79–84.

Weiss, E. H., & Berg, R. F. (1982). Child victims of sexual assault: Impact of court procedures. *Journal of the American Academy of Child Psychiatry, 21,* 513–518.

Whiting, L. (1976). Defining emotional neglect. *Children Today, 5,* 2–5.

Whitten, C. F., Pettit, M. G., & Fischoff, J. (1969). Evidence that growth failure from maternal deprivation is secondary to undereating. *Journal of American Medical Association, 209,* 1675–1682.

Widdowson, E. M. (1951). Mental contentment and physical growth. *Lancet, 1,* 1316–1318.

Widom, L. S., & Ames, M. A. (1994). Criminal consequences of childhood sexual victimization. *Child Abuse and Neglect, 18,* 303–318.

Wilcox, W. D., Nieburg, P., & Miller, D. S. (1989). Failure to thrive: A continuing problem of definition. *Clinical Pediatrics, 28,* 391–394.

Wissow, L. S. (1990). Munchausen by proxy. In L. S. Wissow (Ed.), *Child advocacy for the clinician* (pp. 167–171). Baltimore: Williams & Wilkins.

Wodarski, J., Kurtz, P., Gaudin, J., & Howing, P. (1990). Maltreatment and the school-age child: Major academic, socioemotional and adaptive outcomes. *Social Work, 35,* 506–513.

Wolfe, D. A., Sandler, J., & Kaufman, K. (1981). A competency-based parent training program for child abusers. *Journal of Consulting and Clinical Psychology, 49,* 633–640.

Wolock, I., & Horowitz, B. (1984). Child maltreatment as a social problem: The neglect of neglect. *American Journal of Orthopsychiatry, 54,* 530–543.

Woolley, P. V., & Evans, W. A. (1955). Significance of skeletal lesions in infants resembling those of traumatic origin. *Journal of the American Medical Association, 158,* 539–543.

Wurtele, S., Saslawsky, D., Miller, C., Marrs, S., & Britcher, D. (1988). Teaching personal safety skills for potential prevention of sexual abuse. *Journal of Consulting and Clinical Psychology, 54,* 688–692.

Yates, A. (1981). Narcissistic traits in certain abused children. *Journal of Orthopsychiatry, 51,* 55–62.

Yorukoglu, A., & Kemph, J. P. (1966). Children not severely damaged by incest with a parent. *Journal of the American Academy of Child Psychiatry, 51,* 11–124.

NAME INDEX

SUBJECT INDEX